WHATEVER IT TOOK

WHATEVER IT TOOK

AN AMERICAN PARATROOPER'S EXTRAORDINARY
MEMOIR OF ESCAPE, SURVIVAL, AND HEROISM
IN THE LAST DAYS OF WORLD WAR II

HENRY LANGREHR
AND JIM DeFELICE

WILLIAM MORROW
An Imprint of HarperCollins*Publishers*

A hardcover edition of this book was published in 2020 by William Morrow, an imprint of HarperCollins Publishers.

FIRST WILLIAM MORROW PAPERBACK EDITION PUBLISHED 2021.

Map by the U.S. Army

Library of Congress Cataloging-in-Publication Data has been applied for.

ISBN 978-0-06-302743-5

21 22 23 24 25   LSC   10 9 8 7 6 5 4 3 2

For my family, with great love and affection

Sometimes even to live takes an act of courage.

—Seneca

I am with you always, even unto the end of the world.

—Matthew 28:20

Contents

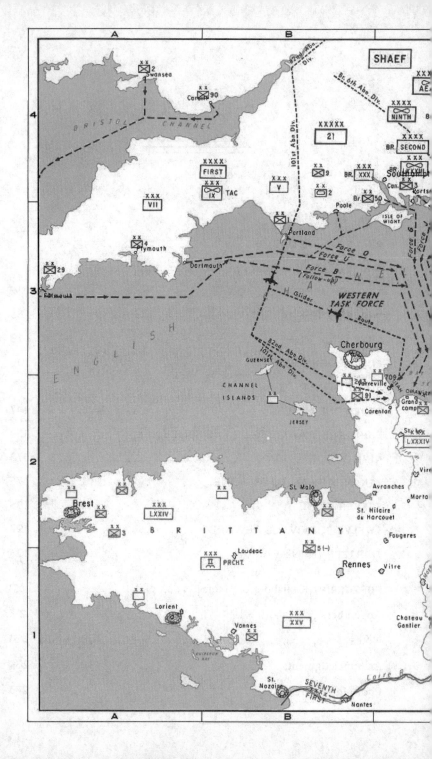

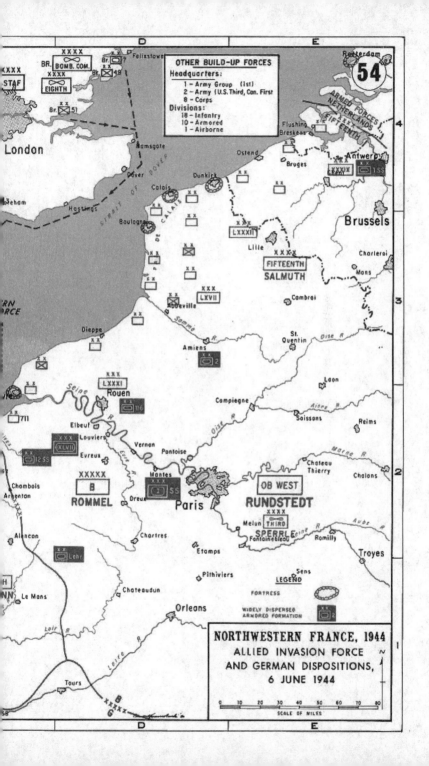

OTHER BUILD-UP FORCES

Headquarters:
1 — Army Group (1st)
2 — Army (U.S. Third, Can. First)
8 — Corps

Divisions:
18 — Infantry
10 — Armored
1 — Airborne

54

LEGEND

FORTRESS

WIDELY DISPERSED
ARMORED FORMATION

NORTHWESTERN FRANCE, 1944
ALLIED INVASION FORCE
AND GERMAN DISPOSITIONS,
6 JUNE 1944

0 10 20 30 40 50 60 70 80
SCALE OF MILES

WHATEVER IT TOOK

Prologue:
VE Day

Tuesday, May 8, 1945: I woke that day a free man, happy beyond belief to be home in America, home in a small house near railroad tracks at the back end of a small city, safe in a tiny, old building that still had no running water or bathroom, but to me was paradise. Not quite a year before, I had jumped from a plane in the wee hours of the morning and landed in the middle of the biggest war mankind has ever known. I'd crashed off target but gotten on with things, helping securing the bridgehead into France.

Many things had happened after that. Horrible things. But in the end, I'd survived.

Now, this morning, May 8, someone was shouting outside—a newsboy hawking papers.

"War is over!" he yelled. "VE Day."

VE Day.

Victory in Europe.

He was wrong. World War II wasn't quite over. We were still fighting the Japanese in the Pacific. But the mistake was understandable. He was excited, and we were all excited. The Germans had surrendered. Adolf Hitler was dead. The bigger part of the conflict was finished. The evil the Nazis had unleashed—evil I'd seen and experienced—had been vanquished. It cost trillions of dollars and countless lives, but it had to be done. Whatever it took, it had to be done.

I stepped outside our little house. Church bells were ringing. Cars beeped. Children and grown men and women played and wept in the streets.

I'd known the war would end for weeks, but still I felt some surprise. Over. It was really over.

Was it? What had happened seemed like a nightmare that had no ending.

I started walking across town, toward my fiancée's home. If I was going to celebrate, it had to be with her.

When we'd met, I was just a teenage child. Now I was a man, a man who'd been to war.

A man who had fought in the hedgerows of France, been shot by a tank, taken prisoner, and interred in a camp where the intent was to work you to death.

A man who had seen the very worst things human beings could do to each other. Who had stood next to the fence of a Nazi death camp and watched the bodies of gassed Jews as they were piled up, then carted away to be burned.

Surviving the war meant living on sawdust and beet juice for months, shivering in a thin blanket in weather so cold your sweat froze. It took beatings so harsh you thought your skull would cave in.

It took choosing almost certain *quick* death over almost certain *slow* death.

It took desperate acts behind enemy lines.

I had learned many things in the year and a half since I'd joined the Army. I learned how to fall out of planes and land without breaking my neck or wrenching my knee. I learned how to blow up bridges, and detect booby traps and mines.

I learned how to navigate in the dark, using stars and dead reckoning. I learned how to survive behind enemy lines, where everyone wants you dead, or worse.

I learned how to kill, and how not to look too deeply into the eyes of the man you shot, for fear of seeing your reflection.

I learned how to become a savage.

I learned how very dark a man's soul can become when he wills himself to survive.

Desperation, hunger, vengeance, and most of all my training as a paratrooper with the U.S. Army's 82nd Airborne made me a fierce warrior—but a reluctant one. Under other circumstances, maybe, I could have been friends with some of the people I had to shoot. But I'd been in a place where I had no friends, and where everyone I met carried my death sentence, no matter how kind their glance seemed.

I tried putting all of that out of my mind as I walked. Today was not a day for deep reflection. Today was a day to celebrate.

VE Day. The war in Europe was over.

ONE

Middle America

CLINTON, IOWA

I am ninety-five years old as I am writing this. There are blanks in my memory now: things I want to remember but can't, names especially. Things I never knew to remember.

There are also things I'd rather forget, but can't.

I will lay it all out here, to the best of my ability, blanks and all.

My childhood was nothing special, for the Depression and middle America. We were poor, and a large family. I'd guess millions of Americans could say about the same thing.

I was born and have lived in Clinton, Iowa, my whole life.

Most people when they think of Iowa imagine vast rows of corn in fields that go on forever, rising from thick clods of black dirt and aiming at an endless sky. That *is* Iowa, but we're also on the border of the Mississippi, and have our share of hills and streams, forests and swamps. In the eastern half of the state, the river remains an essential fact of life.

Lumber was especially important in Clinton's story; they called the city the Lumber Capital of the World. The wood would be sent down the Mississippi and collected here in town. Large rafts of trees were tied together and pushed by boats to the sawmills and woodworking factories. Anything you could think of that could be made of wood was made in one of those factories: furniture, fancy cabinets, doors, window frames, toys. It was good business. I was told there were more millionaires in Clinton than any other small town in America. South Clinton was said to be built on sawdust, the pilings and dredging of the river mixed with the factory leftovers.

By my time, the sawmills had mostly disappeared, but there were still factories around making things from wood. The shops kept a good part of the city employed.

Clinton was a lot like the rest of America, certainly middle America and the Midwest when I was born in 1924—November 4, 1924, to be exact. There were cars, buses, and trucks, but people would walk a mile or two or four and not think too much of it. Not everyone had indoor plumbing—my parents were poor, admittedly, but they didn't get running water until after World War II. I can still remember emptying the chamber pot. We learned what was going on in the world and down the street from newspapers, which would print special editions during the day if something big had happened. Just about everyone, even my parents, had a radio.

TV hadn't been invented, and forget about computers, the internet, or any of that. It would have seemed like Buck Rogers stuff—the science fiction hero from the future who first appeared in the comics in 1929, and movies a little after that.

My family's roots were in Germany, the Hanover area. I'm not sure why my grandparents came over—I've never gone into the family history—but it would have been in the late 1800s. There were a lot of German families already in this part of Iowa. In those days, an immigrant would often be sponsored by someone, either in the family or a friend; the newcomers would work for them or someone they knew at first. Because of that, there were a lot of Germans in the area. My wife's father came in around the time of World War I, maybe just before; her mother, too, was an immigrant, and they only spoke German in the house when she was very small. She didn't learn English until she went to school—imagine having to learn English in kindergarten. But she did just fine.

My mom and dad had ten children, five girls and five boys, though one of the boys died a few months after birth from pneumonia. It was a good-sized family, but I knew families of sixteen. Large families weren't uncommon on the farms; it was a lot of work for the parents, women most of all, but it also meant there were a lot of hands available when needed.

As a kid, my nickname was "Heinie." In some places, the word became a slur after World War I. Children used that word to refer to a certain body part involved in necessary bodily functions. But Heinie was a shortened version of "Heinrich," a very common German name, our "Henry." It had been the nickname of an uncle, and for some reason I don't recall, I inherited it.

My father was a farmhand, and we lived in a small house on the farm. All the kids had chores even when young. The most important ones were carting water in and cutting timber for the kitchen stove, which was the only source of heat in the home.

Marbles were our version of video games. You'd make a circle about three feet around and put a few marbles inside. Then you'd use a "shooter"—a larger marble—to knock others out of the ring. You'd flick the shooter with your thumb, holding it against your forefinger; practice, and you'd get pretty good at getting it to go where you wanted it to go. If your shooter hit a marble out of the circle, you kept that marble and went again. The person with the most marbles when all were out was the winner.

When I was twelve, the city had a summer-long marble competition. Kids all across town competed. Week after week I played and won, filling up bag after bag of marbles. It was quite a collection.

Finally, it came down to just two of us. The championship was a big event—the city newspaper even sent a reporter.

I won. My first and only brush with fame—such as it was.

But I have to confess that I was a bit disappointed when the prize turned out to be a baseball bat and ball. Having spent the entire summer playing, I guess I thought there'd be a bigger prize.

There was probably a lesson there, but I was too young to learn it.

A lot of our spare time was outside, even during the winter. We'd skate, even play ice hockey on the frozen ponds and river inlets that froze over. We'd make our own fun.

If you've ever seen the movie *A Christmas Story*, based on Jean Shepherd's books about his childhood, you probably remember the scene where Ralph's friend gets his tongue stuck on a metal pole thanks to a Triple Dog Dare. The fire department comes to the rescue, but the boy's tongue is quite a bit worse for wear.

Change a few of the circumstances around—no dare was involved—and the same thing happened to me.

A bunch of us boys were talking one day after school, and someone said that their dad told them if you put your tongue on anything metal, it'll freeze to it.

"Aw, that can't be," I told them.

They insisted. I was sure I was right and decided to show them. I went and put my tongue on a pump.

Yes, it did stick.

I peeled it off right away, leaving a bit of tongue on the metal.

Hurt for days.

I didn't tell my parents. In those days, you never told your mom and dad what was going on, at school or at play. That could be asking for trouble. And there wasn't much to be done about my tongue, really; just let it heal. They probably would have laughed their heads off, and told me it served me right.

Another lesson. That one I learned.

DEPRESSION

Most people have heard about Black Friday, the crash of the New York Stock Market that marked the start of the Great Depression. For my family, the Depression began with a local bank failure a little afterward. The collapse of the bank completely wiped out my father's savings—$1,200. Right alongside that, jobs suddenly became hard to find. Those there were paid less than they had. Everybody was hurting. Farms went under. People lost their houses.

With no farm work, my family moved to a house near the railroad tracks where the rent was lower. We were about twenty feet off the tracks; everything rattled and shook when the big trains came through. But at least one good thing came out of that: I can sleep like a baby no matter what's going on around me.

For ten years in there, we didn't have money for much of anything except rent and food, maybe, and sometimes not even that. It's hard for people to realize how bad it was. You worked as much as you could. Large families had many people to contribute, but that also meant more mouths to feed. Going to bed hungry was not unusual. We spent one summer living in a tent, I suppose to save on rent.

I've always figured that God brought that Depression because he knew in the end it would be a good training for us. We could do hardship.

My father started a business collecting what some might call junk—old tractors and whatnot, most of which didn't work. He'd fix the tractors up and sell them. He must not have made much from that, since there wouldn't have been many people who could buy anything, even used equipment. But he made do.

The tractors I remember were big contraptions, steam-powered. There was a thresher or two as well. My father would also make money by taking the scrap metal over to Morris Turner at Turner Iron & Metal, who'd weigh it and pay by the pound. A few cents and dollars meant the family could eat for another week.

I did that job when I got a bit older. I'd take one of my younger brothers—I was the second oldest—and we'd drag a cart up to be weighed. Mr. Turner was a nice old fellow, and if he realized my little brother was sneaking onto the scale to add a few pennies to our haul, he never mentioned it.

Franklin Delano Roosevelt was elected in 1932, promising to start some programs to get people back to work. My father got a job on one. It was good, honest work, and you can still see some of the results. He helped build a few buildings, worked on stone walls, and was part of the crew paving Highway 67, which is still an important road in the area.

Things were a bit better for our family while the work lasted; we didn't starve. Still, the winters were cold and the nights long. The days often weren't too much better. We had to move a few times because we couldn't pay the rent. But we always seemed to end up near the railroad tracks.

One of our homes was across from the county jail. Most of the people in there at the time were drunks who were drying out. You'd hear them singing in the summer when the windows were open, and see them on work duty cutting grass around town or doing other odd jobs. We'd play in the empty lot, sneaking glances at them—curious, but not wanting to be like them, either. I don't know that they were the reason that I never drank much, but if I needed an example of what alcohol could do to you, there they were.

Baseball was a favorite of ours, and probably with most of the boys across the country. It really was the national pastime then. I played when I could, but as I grew older that was less and less. I was too busy working to try out for the school team, and gradually lost interest. I don't even follow the Chicago teams much these days.

The family garden supplied a lot of food during the summer and well into the winter. Even the littlest kids would have chores to do in the garden, raking in the spring to break up the soil, weeding and watering as the plants grew. Come last summer and early fall, my mother would put up vegetables. She also canned chickens and ducks that we kept, something not so common for home cooks now. One winter I remember something went wrong with the canning and all the chicken spoiled—a bitter, hungry loss.

Kids would walk along the railroad tracks, looking for coal that had fallen from the trains passing through. A lot of that coal had help "falling"—older kids and even young men would climb on the train cars as they slowed through town, then kick as much coal off as they could. We'd run and grab some before they hopped off and came to collect it themselves. You didn't want them to catch you doing it; we were a lot more afraid of them than the railroad people.

There was also a gas works in town, which made gas from the coal. They would throw the ashes in the town dump; you could scavenge through the refuse and find a few unburned lumps of coal or coke. Anything to stay warm.

When I was twelve years old, I bought a six-shot Ranger shotgun from Sears. It was eleven dollars, and the shells were twenty-two cents apiece. Big money back then, but it was a good weapon—I still have it today. It was 16 gauge—not so common anymore.

That was my first gun. I taught myself to use it, and hunted up in the fields above town, where the dam is now. There were farms in there before the dams were built and they had ponds on them where the ducks and geese congregated. I'd go with my friends and get so many ducks you couldn't hardly carry them home. Rabbits and even raccoons that came along—all food.

We'd fish, too. It was all a matter of feeding the family. We didn't have the fancy gear they have now, just a cane pole, a hook, and line. But there were so many fish in the shallow backwaters that we'd just wade out with a net, you know, wade out and get all kinds of fish. Either there were more fish, or maybe they were just dumber back then.

There was also a time when they were paying twenty-five cents a pelt for racoons. So hunting was food and money . . . and a little fun.

There was a hobo camp in the woods north of the city, near a railroad bridge that wasn't far from our house. We kids would go up sometimes and see what was going on. Usually, not much. The men would hop off a train, look around town for work or food, maybe stay a few days, and then be off. They were even more desperate than we were.

One time a friend was having a birthday party and invited me. I didn't have anything to give as a present. He said that was all right, just come.

It turned out he liked to box, and his father did, too. They had a ring set up. They had invited me to fight. I guess they thought I'd be an easy mark.

I didn't want to fight. They kept pushing me. I didn't want to be a sissy, so finally I fought.

I bloodied my friend's nose. His father sent me home, angry I guess because I'd beaten him.

I hadn't wanted to fight in the first place. It wasn't who I was.

At fourteen I started looking for more formal work outside the house, beginning by cutting grass with a small push mower. I had two prices—ten cents for a small lawn; twenty-five for a bigger one. Trimming the hedges cost another twenty cents; if you wanted the debris hauled to the city dump rather than dumped in the alley or backyard, we'd negotiate a price. That went for hauling ashes and other items as well.

In the winter, a good snow could net me fifty cents when I cleared a walkway. That was for a large stretch of anything over five inches deep; lesser storms and smaller paths paid less.

Whatever I got went straight to the family. At times my father was making no more than six dollars a week, with rent running twelve dollars a month. On such a budget, a large snowfall could be a godsend.

Understanding how poor you are is a strange thing. As a young kid, I had little to judge myself against. My friends all ran barefoot in the summer; it felt good—free, even. If it was necessary to save on shoes, that wasn't the sort of thing that a kid quite understood.

But there were times when circumstance and people's prejudices came together to make it clear that not only didn't we have money, but that others looked down on us. My eighth-grade graduation was one such time. Grammar school graduation was a very formal and important affair; the end of eighth grade meant the end of schooling for a lot of people. We were supposed to wear our best clothes to the ceremony, white dresses for the girls, dark pants and white shirts for the boys.

I had no white shirt, nor what would be considered a good pair of pants. The teachers told me I couldn't take part in the ceremony; I watched from the audience.

Lacking good clothes didn't keep me from going to high school. Or from working.

The summer after tenth grade, I applied at a local toy factory. They told me I was too young.

I kept going back, and finally they decided to give me a job sweeping up sawdust, hauling trash, and the like—as long as I kept away from the saws and other heavy machinery. The following year, those restrictions were lifted. I also got a job working as an usher in a movie theater—there were three in town. So I'd go to school, go to the theater, and then on to the factory. That had me working until 11 P.M. many nights.

Other jobs followed. I was always working. I remember getting twenty-five cents an hour at a food processing company loading refrigerator train cars with butter and eggs. I was happy for the work, and happier still that I was helping the family survive.

———————

Religion didn't play a big part in my life. In fact, it played no part. While both of my parents were German, they had come from different branches of Christianity—my dad Lutheran, my mom Catholic. Maybe because of that, they didn't take us to church, and I can't say that I knew much about God. In fact, I only remember going to church once as a child, when I was around ten. A friend said that his church gave out candy and fruit after the Christmas service; naturally I accepted his invitation to tag along.

I can't remember a word the pastor said, but the sweetness of the apples, oranges, and candy remains fixed in my memory.

———————

Though I was working hard, my grades didn't seem to suffer. I did okay in class.

The economy was slowly improving. Things seemed headed in

a good direction. Then came a shock that changed my future, and that of everyone around me.

INFAMY AND LOVE

The world had been at war both in Asia and Europe for several years. Japan attacked Manchuria, China, in 1931; in 1937, the Japanese launched a full-scale invasion of north central China, quickly taking over Beijing; Shanghai fell a few months later. While the Japanese occupied much of the coast and the area of Vietnam, guerrilla resistance and regular fighting continued.

Meanwhile in Europe, Adolf Hitler and the Nazis rose to power. Germany annexed Austria, marched into Czechoslovakia, and in 1939 invaded Poland. France and Great Britain, allies of Poland, declared war. Germany invaded France in 1940, quickly taking over the country. A bombing campaign targeting British cities as well as military bases followed.

Isolated by two large oceans, most Americans felt the wars were distant. They were too far away to ever affect us. Certainly as a high school student, I paid very little attention to the conflicts.

And then the Japanese bombed Pearl Harbor. The oceans seemed to shrink that Sunday afternoon, and so did the idea of my future. I wasn't looking forward to fighting or becoming a soldier, but now I knew both were very real possibilities.

As a high school student, not yet old enough to be drafted or even volunteer, I had more immediate concerns: school, work . . . and a budding romance.

Blame the last on fly swatters.

In the winter of 1943, I'd just turned nineteen and was still in high school. I began working at a fly swatter factory. My job was to drill the hole in the handle so the swatter could be hung from a hook. I happened to work right next to the station where felt edging was placed around the frame and netting. This geography happened to introduce me to a young lady by the name of Arlene Ketelsen, who sewed the edging.

Arlene was very pretty, and an older woman . . . by a few months. Our shifts did not exactly align; I would typically leave not long after she arrived, but our brief encounters were enough to stir my heart.

But not my tongue. I was too shy to ask her out, even after confessing to a friend and coworker that I was a bit interested in her. When my friend suggested I take her on a date, I found an excuse; after a few such mumbles he decided to play Cupid himself. He tricked me into going to the movies, arranged for Arlene to come, and somehow we ended up on a double date.

Best little trick anyone ever played on me.

Here was another little trick, this one not so pleasant—though it's funny to think back on it now. I knew Arlene's address, and I knew the street where she lived. What I didn't know was that the houses were numbered in an odd way on the street, a bit out of order, and if you weren't looking very hard for the house, it was easy to miss.

In fact, even if you were looking hard, you might miss it. Which is what happened to me the first time I went to meet her at her house. I walked down the street, checking off the numbers in my head as I went.

No luck.

Hmmm. Must've missed it.

I went back, counting again.

Nope.

I must have walked back and forth a dozen times before I finally found the house, hiding in plain sight.

What I didn't know was that Arlene, alerted by one of her brothers, was watching the whole time. She won't admit this now, but I think my determination to find that house was one of the things that attracted her to me.

Arlene's family was also German. Her father, Karl, had come to America as a young man; he'd worked out west as a cowboy on a ranch, then moved eastward and eventually to the Clinton area as a farmhand. During Prohibition, they grew corn and turned it into whiskey, selling to fellows from Chicago in big cars who paid in cash money, and well—we think that means he was a bootlegger and part of the famous mobster Al Capone's network, but who knows?

Karl put down roots in Clinton, marrying and raising a large family with his wife, Amanda, a local girl. But the Depression was as tough on them as it was on our family. The farm Karl worked on failed; the family moved into town, where he bought enough land to grow vegetables and raise chickens. With seven kids to keep warm during the long Iowa winters, Karl put a back room on his two-room house and set a heating stove inside. All nine of them would bunk down there each night, their feet warmed by bricks wrapped in towels. The kids would bring in money by collecting berries before school and selling them. Curtains and clothes were fashioned from large bags of flour once their contents had been used.

Even after Karl found work in a factory, things were still tight for his family. Then, just before I met Arlene, Karl suffered a bout of rheumatism so bad that he couldn't walk. He stayed at home in bed for ten months, unable to earn any money. Arlene's mother got a job; Arlene, the only girl in the family, helped by taking care of the youngest children until she, too, was old enough to work outside the home. Meanwhile, her grandmother ran a boarding-house, letting rooms to railroad workers and others.

After the local bank failure, few people trusted banks at all, even for loans. Arlene's grandmother got the money to buy the house from a local businessman. He prefaced each month's request for the mortgage with a question: "Gussy, can you feed your children?"

He didn't want to take the money if the extended family's kids were starving.

———————

Arlene and I started dating. The dates weren't much—a movie, maybe, but mostly walks and just spending time together. When you are young and in love you don't need much.

By this time, the war was going full blast. A lot of my friends were leaving school to join the service. I knew I would be drafted, and so I decided I would join up and pick the service I wanted, rather than just being assigned.

I chose the Merchant Marine, which transported supplies overseas in ships. It was dangerous work. German U-boats were prowling the oceans between America, Great Britain, and Russia. Russia, then known as the Soviet Union, had joined the war as an ally of Great Britain in the summer of 1941, when Germany invaded the country in violation of a nonaggression agreement. The Germans had been stopped just outside of Moscow, at a huge loss of life. By early 1943, a large part of the eastern half of the Soviet Union was under German control.

Sailors who worked on the ships were not actually part of the Navy; technically they were civilian volunteers though they played an important part in the conflict. Besides the possibility of being sunk by subs or attacked by planes and ships, they braved extreme cold on the far northern sea routes and the usual dangers of the sea. But I'd heard that the pay was pretty good—$800 to $1,000 per trip—and that the sailors could receive bonuses higher than what soldiers would receive, which meant I could help my still-struggling family.

As for the danger, it didn't really register with me. I'd been through so much hardship growing up that I thought little about it.

The fact that I knew nothing about being a sailor didn't make much difference to me, either. I told them I wanted to work on engines. I had no direct experience with the diesels that ran ships, but I'd tinkered with my share of tractor motors and figured I could learn easily enough.

You'd think they would be tickled to have someone volunteer to work down in the grimiest, darkest, stinkiest part of the ship. The compartment not only farthest from the lifeboats, but almost always the very last to be abandoned when the ship was going down.

Maybe the recruiters I met were jumping for joy, but they still told me I'd have to wait a few weeks until they had an opening.

———————

That seemed like an eternity. Once I make up my mind to do something, I'm ready to do it. So I looked around for another branch, and settled on the Army's paratroopers. I had never been in an airplane—let alone jumped out of one. But I'd read some-where about them being the latest fighting thing, an extremely capable group of elite fighting men. The idea of being in with the best of the best excited me.

And let me be completely honest: The fact that paratroopers would be paid extra—I think it was fifty dollars a month on top of regular pay—didn't hurt, either.

So I signed up. They gave me a physical, checked my eyes—you needed good vision to qualify, which made sense but surprised me—and gave me a green light. As long as I finished the training, I was in.

Failure would mean the "regular" Army. A fine institution, but as far as I was concerned, failure was not going to happen.

———————

Arlene and I had been going out for only a few weeks, but it was still hard to say good-bye. I didn't know it yet, but I was already deeply in love. As I boarded the bus and waved to her I felt a twinge of something I'd never felt before. I didn't regret volunteering, but I also knew there was something more I wanted from life than fighting and the Army.

It was a different sort of experience for Arlene. Not only was she saying good-bye to me, but she was meeting my parents for the first time. Her relationship with my mother was distant at best, but my father was a different sort all together. He was cold, even to me. I never got a hug; he just didn't show his emotions. I've always thought that it had to do with his family background; on the whole, German families can be very rigid and unemotional.

On the other hand, Arlene's family was German as well, and almost the complete opposite. So take my theory with a grain of salt.

My feelings for Arlene went on hold for the next few weeks as

I was indoctrinated into the U.S. Army at Camp Dodge in Johnston, Iowa. North of Des Moines in the center of the state, about 185 miles due west of Clinton, today it's about a three-hour car ride along Interstate 80. But it felt as if it were on a different continent. It was the farthest I'd ever been from home, far different than Clinton.

Army life was rigorous, but in some ways better than what I'd experienced growing up. There was plenty of food, and as long as you did your job and followed the rules, it was easy to get along. In the little spare time I had, I wrote a lot of letters back to Arlene. She'd send packs of home-baked cookies; no food I ever had in the Army ever compared.

Like every other volunteer and draftee, my introduction to army life was basic training. "Basic," as we called it, was just that—a very simple introduction to Army ways and the basics of being a soldier. When I finished, I was selected to be a combat engineer with the paratroops.

"Combat engineer" may sound like the job of someone who designs or builds bridges and buildings. In fact, it was more the opposite, at least for me—most of what I was taught was how to blow things up. We learned how to destroy bridges, rig TNT, and make improvised bombs. We were also instructed in how to disarm mines and similar booby traps. In short, training turned us into demolitions experts.

That was in addition to the more normal role of a paratrooper, who was trained to jump out of airplanes and fight behind enemy lines. Combat engineers were formed into their own companies, which were then attached and integrated into larger parachute units. Assignments and actual arrangements varied according to need, but in theory if a bridge behind enemy lines needed to be destroyed, combat engineers would be given that task.

The first stage in this training was at Camp Cooke in California. Known today as Vandenberg Air Force Base, Cooke was a massive facility near the California coast, not quite midway between Los Angeles and San Francisco. It had a variety of roles during the war—it even served as a POW camp for German and Italian prisoners. The vast ranges included plenty of places where we could blow things up without too much damage to ourselves or others.

Besides gaining these skills, we were toughening our bodies. We started by hiking five miles. Gradually that was increased to twenty-five. As a paratrooper fighting behind the lines, you had to rely on your body. It needed to be strong to survive; endurance was mandatory. We pushed ourselves a little farther every day, trusting that the pain we might endure would pay off down the line.

When my training at Cooke was complete, I was given two weeks to get to Fort Benning in Georgia, where I would learn how to jump out of airplanes. Those two weeks amounted to a vacation, and I made use of them to stop home and see Arlene.

I can't remember now exactly how much time I spent with her, but it was enough to get the courage to ask her to marry me.

Yes! She said yes.

She took quite a chance saying yes. By the summer of 1943, America was deeply involved in World War II. Things were going far better than they had in 1942, but the outcome of the war was far from decided. It was obvious that a lot more fighting was at hand.

The Allies had succeeded in kicking Germany out of northern Africa, liberated Sicily, and in September 1943 invaded southern Italy. But making progress in Italy proved to be very difficult. Mussolini was deposed and arrested by the new government—only to be rescued and reinstated by Hitler.

German troops took over the defense of Italy. They made excellent use of the mountainous terrain, stalling the Allies' advance and inflicting large casualties.

On the Eastern Front between Germany and the Soviet Union, the Russian Red Army routed the invaders in an epic, months-long battle at Stalingrad. That fight alone saw as many as 1.1 million Russians and 900,000 Germans and assorted allies killed, wounded, or taken prisoner; 40,000 civilians were killed as well. While the battle is seen today as a turning point in the war, that was not obvious to us at the time. Even to the people paying attention, it could easily be viewed as one win in a string of failures.

The war in the Pacific had its own unrecognized turning point that year at the Battle of Midway. A large Japanese force had been met by American aircraft carriers. The Japanese navy lost four aircraft carriers and a large number of planes and experienced pilots; it would never be the same—though we had no way of knowing that back home. Instead, anyone following the news of the different island campaigns fought by the Navy, Marines, and Army might be puzzled: day-to-day accounts made the war in the Pacific look like a seesaw affair, not a steady progress toward an inevitable end.

If you asked most people in 1943 when a turning point in the war might come, at least in Europe, many might have mentioned liberating France. The dramatic German takeover of the country in 1940 had been shocking, an almost unimaginable rearranging of the world order. Ever since joining the war, America and Great Britain had planned to invade France and liberate it; the Soviet Union's premier, Joseph Stalin, had been arguing for a large-scale invasion to open a "second front" on the continent for just as long. Plans for just such an invasion were already well under way, though of course I knew nothing of that when I boarded the train to head for Fort Benning. I didn't even know, not really, how the war was going. Being just a kid at nineteen, I was sure we were going to win, but I never could have outlined what it would take. I may not even have known all the places American troops were fighting.

I did know I had to get Arlene a diamond ring. And that I had to survive not only training but the rest of the war.

I may have had a few doubts. Arlene had none. She told me then—and many times since—that she knew I would make it home from the war. She just knew.

The train was crowded with GIs going to different assignments on the East Coast.

The America we saw from the train was very different than the country we would have seen a decade before during the depth of the Great Depression. There were still farms and fields, cities and factories, but they were far busier. Smoke poured out of the stacks of industrial plants that had turned from idleness or civilian production to making the tools necessary to conduct war in the modern era—everything from bootlaces to aircraft.

In the worst of the Depression, the country's industry and trade had shrunk to roughly half what it had been in 1920; now it was triple that or even more.

Fort Benning, Georgia, was home to the Army's airborne training school. They toughened you up first thing—out of bed at 0500 or 5 A.M., march fifteen miles day one, then eighteen, then twenty-one, twenty-five . . . Learn first aid, cooking, navigating—everything you needed to know behind the lines.

But the most important thing you learned was how to jump out of an airplane.

You started with learning how to land. Fall and roll—something you took for granted, I guess, if you'd ever roughhoused with your brothers or friends. Things quickly went from there.

There was a drill where we slid down a line from shacks made up to look like a small section of an airplane, landing in sawdust about as hard as you would land on an actual jump. Wind machines—big fans—were used on the ground to give you the feel of controlling and stowing your parachute when you landed.

Towers got us used to falling a few hundred feet; you started at forty feet and went up to two hundred and fifty feet—at least that's what they said; I didn't have a ruler with me at the time. According to legend at the field, the towers had been taken from the parachute rides at the 1939 World's Fair in New York, amusement rides that duplicated the experience of jumping from a plane.

Now, whether that's really where they came from, I have no idea. I will also tell you that using the towers was nothing like jumping out of an airplane. But we had to start somewhere.

Rising over two-story buildings at their base, the towers were made of metal girders like the massive structures used for electrical lines. Four long arms spread out in an X at the top. You and a buddy would be hoisted to the top, then descend under a parachute attached to guide wires. It was a lot more amusement park than airplane—assuming you'd gone to the amusement park in uniform and jump boots.

People ask if I was scared that first time. I guess I had the right to be. A few fellows were. And I'd never been that high in my life. Oh, I'd climbed my share of trees, and I'd ridden a carnival ride or two, but nothing came close to those towers.

I wasn't scared. Just the opposite. I loved pretty much every second of it.

Why?

I'm not sure. I'd never been afraid of heights. For some reason I just looked at it as an adventure, and fun. Maybe I thought it was just a carnival ride. For whatever reason, it was fun. I couldn't wait for more.

After a few days of these different drills, we graduated to the real thing—a one-way trip off the airfield in a C-47 aircraft.

My first time ever in a plane, and I wasn't even going to get to land in it.

The C-47 Skytrain—the official designation—was derived from the civilian DC-3 airline. The door was toward the back of the aircraft, on the side of the fuselage; when you went out, you could feel the wash of the engines. Besides the four-man crew, the aircraft could carry twenty-eight passengers. Geared-up paratroopers, who might be carrying seventy or more pounds, were a heavy load, just within (and sometimes beyond) its specs. The two Pratt & Whitney R-1830 Twin Wasp engines on the military versions delivered 1,200 horsepower at full rev for takeoff. It was no speed demon; at 10,000 feet, its rated maximum speed was 225 knots or nautical miles per hour; compare that to a fighter that was fast—the P-51 Mustang, for example—and you'll find the much smaller Mustang could go two hundred knots faster.

But the C-47 wasn't built for speed. It was an extremely dependable and versatile aircraft, used not only by the United States but most of our allies, in both the European and Pacific campaigns of the war.

The DC-3 had first flown in 1935. When the war came, a number of civilian aircraft were converted for military use, but the bulk were made with the small number of military modifications already worked in. More than ten thousand were built for the service; others were made overseas under license. Few other planes can come close to its record of service.

I was nervous the first time I boarded the aircraft; I expect everyone was. We told a lot of jokes back and forth to hide it. Once we were airborne and the wind started whipping through the open door, the jokes died down.

This is going to be fun, I thought. Like a circus ride.

There were fifteen of us in the "stick," or group, of paratroopers assigned to leave the plane. I was toward the back—number 11. I waited for what seemed like an eternity as the plane taxied and took off. Time seemed to pass both slowly and quickly, if that's possible.

Finally we reached altitude, somewhere between eight hundred and a thousand feet on that first jump. The jumpmaster rose and began bellowing. He was a medium-sized fellow, but he had the voice of a giant, more than loud enough to be heard over the drone of the engines and the rush of the wind.

His tone wasn't all that friendly.

Up and at 'em!

Go!

Now!

I said, NOW!

We made two lines, one from each side of the plane. The men nearest the door stood first. Each took the strap that attached to his parachute and hooked its end onto a cable that ran like a spine down the ceiling of the fuselage.

The hook ran smoothly along the cable as you walked toward the door. When you went out, it would pull open the parachute—static line jumping.

The static line ran fifteen feet, a half breath or so as you fell. The canopy of the parachute measured twenty-eight feet, with twenty-eight cells; it gave you a pretty decent jerk when it opened some twenty-two feet above your head.

You also had a reserve or emergency parachute attached to your front. This had a handle that could be pulled if the main chute failed; the reserve would then blossom and save you.

You tried not to think about that the first time you jumped. Or maybe anytime.

I remember I counted the number of steps to the door; if my memory is correct, it was exactly forty.

On this first trial, each man seemed to pause when he reached the doorway. He'd hold on for dear life and ask himself, *Do I really want to do this?*

Can I do this?

Or maybe not ask anything at all, just observe:

Boy, that's a long way down.

When it was my turn at the door, I stopped, too, took a breath, had a look, thought about that imaginary circus ride, and then just went. Everything else was and remains a blur.

The static line tightened and pulled out the chute. The jolt shocked and surprised me. The draft from the engine surprised me. The wind and gravity surprised me.

And then I was falling, pretty gently, held up in the sky by silk and air. I was part of a speckled cloud of men suspended beneath round canopies bobbing in the airstream, tugged downward by gravity.

It was a thrill.

A fantastic thrill. Better than any circus ride I'd been on, seen, or even imagined.

Those words don't begin to explain what I felt. It was joy. It was the thrill of being free. It was the excitement of being pumped up. It was adrenaline. It was knowing you had just lived through a huge thrill when you landed. It was accomplishment. It was every bone in your body, every muscle, every hair, vibrating with electricity.

I loved parachuting from my first jump, and soon started doing it as much as I could, in formal and informal exercises. I learned to jump with full gear. I learned to jump from different altitudes. I learned to jump at night, something I never particularly liked, since darkness robbed you of most markers you could use to steer or prepare for the shock of touchdown. I learned how to lay myself out as soon as I hit the slipstream, how to steer with my risers, how to deal with emergencies. I found out that "rolling" on landing when you were wearing all your gear was a bit of a joke;

no way could you find any sort of balance, let alone grace and co-ordination, with all that added weight.

I still loved it. Maybe even more.

But it wasn't for everyone. I remember that three men backed out of the door during that first exercise; I think they left air-borne and joined other units. You could back out without penalty until you completed your fifth jump; at that point, you were of-ficially a paratrooper—and refusing to jump would get you court-martialed, or so I was told.

Parachuting was very intense, but it was really a very small part of our job in the 82nd. As paratroopers, we had to learn to fight behind enemy lines, and to do it without the normal support reg-ular infantry units would have—big tanks, heavy artillery, and rich lines of supply. We learned to fight in small groups, assault-ing enemy units. We were taught to navigate through unfamiliar territory using maps and compasses, and sometimes just the stars and our own wits.

At the same time, we worked to build up our endurance. This meant hiking—and a lot of it. Generally this would be with full combat equipment; you'd have forty or more pounds in your rucksack and full pockets of gear and ammo. A typical exercise might set you out on a fifteen-mile hike. We didn't just walk those miles; we'd run fifteen minutes every hour before reaching our objective.

The next day, a truck would pick up your company and drive twenty miles from the barracks. *Okay, boys,* the driver would say. *We'll see you back home.*

So we'd learn how to navigate and march, building brain and brawn together.

The next day we'd do it again, or maybe take part in a war game, pitting us against another unit. Stealthy attack against a larger opponent became second nature.

Then there were the obstacle courses, climbing, jumping, running. We climbed ropes, up and down. We ran.

And then we marched again.

Blisters on your feet from your toes rubbing against the boots and socks were a common, constant problem. They could get real bad, but you didn't want to fall out or report them because it could cost you your chance. Marching was part of the job—and not just for paratroopers. Even a mechanized, mobile soldier spends an inordinate amount of time working the soles of his feet against the ground. You learned to suck it up—or in the language of today's soldiers, you learned to revel in the suck.

One thing you could count on—fatigue. We'd be woken up at one or two in the morning and hustled out for a march or exercise. Maybe it would be raining. Somehow our bodies adapted to the constant abuse. Our instructors were trying to duplicate the conditions we might find in war. They did everything they could think of except shoot at us.

The numbers are hazy now, but I think my "class" of engineers at Benning started with thirty or even forty guys; by the time we graduated in January 1944, there were only a dozen. I still have my diploma from Parachute School, a framed certificate on the wall of my office declaring I am one of a rare brotherhood: permitted to wear "chutists" wings and tuck my pants cuffs into my boots, the unofficial mark of a true paratrooper.

After Benning, I went to Fort Bragg in North Carolina for further training. I was now a private first class, PFC, and demolition specialist, with qualifications as expert with a rifle and carbine (at the time, separate distinctions). I was assigned to Company B of the 307th Parachute Engineers Battalion, part of the 505th Regimental Combat Team, which itself was part of the 82nd Airborne.

I usually just mention my assignment as the 82nd. Saves time, and it's a unit people know.

———————

As I said, my job in 1944 was different than what may first come to mind when you hear the word "engineer." I was destroying things, not putting them together. The Army's Corps of Engineers were tasked with a wide range of projects, from building airfields to repairing ports. In my case, my job would be pretty much the same as a "regular" paratrooper, trained to jump behind enemy lines and then fight there for days or weeks, as long as necessary.

I carried a Thompson submachine, which could be broken down and attached to my chest when I jumped. The Thompson was affectionately known as a "Tommy gun," and was the gangster's weapon of choice during the Prohibition era. It fired a lot of bullets very quickly and made quite a racket doing so—just the sort of thing you want if you're in the bad-guy business, or better yet, making a movie about it. We learned to be more selective, firing a few bullets at a time. You needed to control the weapon and, especially when you were cut off from support, conserve your ammo.

The Thompson we saw on the movie screens had a round drum for its bullets. Ours had a straight magazine. But otherwise it was the same, designed to be used at comparatively close quarters. I also carried a .45 Colt semiautomatic pistol. The Thompson and the Colt used the same caliber bullets, which made things a little simpler and lighter.

One piece of equipment made me stand out from other paratroopers, even to an untrained, civilian eye: when I jumped from a plane in combat, I had a large (and heavy) satchel tied to my leg. The bag contained the work tools of a combat engineer, things like blasting caps and explosives.

In February 1944, the Army decided I was ready for the war. I headed up to Camp Shanks in New York, where I boarded the *Queen Elizabeth* and sailed for Great Britain. I weighed 150 pounds and stood between five-feet-four and five-six—a little below average height, but well built and ready to fight. I had spent nearly a year training to become an elite fighter, part of a growing force gaining momentum in a bloody war. I felt ready for anything, and I'd venture to say that most of the other soldiers on that big liner felt the same way.

We had a lot to learn.

TWO

Training Up

DEVILS

When the naval architects at the Cunard Line drew her up, the RMS *Queen Elizabeth* was intended as one of the finest ships afloat, the sister of the equally fabulous *Queen Mary*. A touch bigger than the *Mary*, *Elizabeth* measured 1,031 feet from bow to stern, and displaced approximately 83,000 tons. Her polished-wood cabins and less fancy berths would host more than two thousand passengers; her crew might add another thousand. In the days before intercontinental air travel was common, the *Queen Elizabeth* was destined to be both a star and a workhorse, ferrying passengers of all classes between Europe and America.

Then came World War II. Though she had been christened, *Elizabeth* was not yet completely fitted out. Very few civilians wanted to brave the hostile submarines, warships, and aircraft prowling the Atlantic, and the liner seemed destined to sit indefinitely in the shipyard.

That would have been an immense waste. If civilians weren't

looking to get to Europe anytime soon, GIs were. And so the ship was put into service as one of the world's largest, fastest, and most luxurious troopships ever.

There were only hints of luxury when I boarded her at the end of February. The large dining hall and elaborate stairways remained, but otherwise the ship appeared drab and overcrowded. Oh, she was chock-full of people. Her exterior had been painted gray; her interior smelled not so much of the sea but the sweat of thousands of troops headed for war. I'm not sure how many soldiers were aboard on my voyage; typical winter cruises carried between ten thousand and twelve thousand men, but I'd believe even more. We were bunched together like sardines in a can. Cabins where two people would have been snug were now outfitted with special bunks; eight men were assigned in each. The ship's large dining spaces couldn't come close to holding us all; we had to eat in shifts. I'd grab my food, wolf it down, then squeeze through the crowd to escape up to the deck and fresh air.

It wasn't much of an escape—the deck was usually crowded as well. We were supposed to wear a life belt at all times; we were also supposed to keep to certain areas of the ship, mostly to lessen some of the overcrowding. Just out of New York, we conducted a boat drill, with everyone heading for the lifeboat. Call it somewhat controlled chaos; imagine the crowd at a baseball game funneling into a space narrower than the diamond and you'll get the idea.

At flank speed—that's "all out" for us landlubbers—the ship could hit 28 knots and maybe a few more. That made it one of the fastest if not the fastest ship crossing the Atlantic. It could easily outrun a submerged or even surfaced submarine. Unlike most transports, the *Queen* traveled alone, her gray silhouette streaking across the ocean like a speeding ghost.

I can't remember now how long the trip took; generally it was five or six days, and I would guess our passage was about the same. The trip seemed routine; then again, this was my first time on a ship, so I had nothing to compare it to. We arrived in Belfast, Ireland, then moved to a base nearby.

While I would end up functioning as a kind of "free agent" working with "regular" paratroopers, I was assigned to the 307th Parachute Engineers Battalion. The 307th was part of the 505th Regimental Combat Team (RCT), one of three such teams that made up the 82nd Airborne, the Army's first paratrooper division. Airborne RCTs were built around a paratrooper regiment and combined units of different specialties, all training and working together as a unit. The core of our RCT was the 505th Parachute Infantry Regiment, by then a storied and well-blooded outfit.

Paratroopers were a very new part of warfare, but the basic idea behind them was ancient: surprise the enemy by attacking where you were least expected. It was the same sort of idea that Hannibal used when he marched elephants over the Alps to attack the Romans. The Germans used paratroopers during the early, blitzkrieg stages of the war, dropping the men behind enemy lines ahead of their advancing forces. They operated as commandoes, attacking lightly defended posts and holding strategic points until the advancing ground armies could reach them. The Germans also used paratroopers and gliders in large formations to take over the island of Crete in May 1941; here they were the main assault force, deployed as regular troops might be, once on the ground.

No matter how they were used, paratroopers were considered

an elite force, specially trained not just to parachute but to fight. That's why so much of my training, and the rest of the unit's, centered around what are called "small group tactics" in the Army. We learned to engage the enemy in multiple ways, usually without support. And to do it behind enemy lines. Even though my specialty was blowing things up, I was expected to be able to do it for days and even weeks if necessary, without an officer or even a sergeant directing me.

Heady stuff for a nineteen-year-old.

In our Army, airborne troops traced their origins to World War I, when the 82nd Division fought in France. Then strictly a ground unit, its infantrymen took part in severe fighting around Saint-Mihiel and the Moselle River in September 1918; Colonel Emory Jenison Pike of the 321st Machine Gun Battalion was awarded the Medal of Honor for valor following the battle. Later in the month, it fought in the Meuse-Argonne offensive, the Allies' surge that ended the war. Alvin York, the most famous World War I soldier, won a medal of honor for his actions in the campaign, including his capture of 132 German prisoners while armed with a pistol.

The 82nd was nicknamed the "All American" division because it included soldiers drafted from all across America—not the usual arrangement at the time, with many units starting as National Guard units, created in the states. After the war, it became part of the reserve, spread out between South Carolina, Georgia, and Florida. With the declaration of war, the 82nd was taken out of the reserves and began training as a regular infantry unit, headed by Omar Bradley. Among the officers on his staff were men who would play a large role in the war.

When the Army decided to devote an entire division to airborne, it picked the 82nd; evaluators considered it one of if not the best-trained and -prepared divisions in the Army. It would eventually help seed another division—the 101st—and become one of the most decorated units fighting in Europe. Two other divisions of airborne—the 11th, fighting in the Pacific, and the 17th, which joined us later in Europe—were stood up before the end of the war. Another division, the 15th, was authorized but was not activated.

Besides two Parachute Infantry Regiments, the 82nd included a Glider Infantry Regiment, two Glider Field Artillery Battalions, two Field Artillery Battalions, an Airborne Anti-Aircraft Battalion, a medical company, and combat engineers—my 307th. Other troops were assigned at different points, along with a third regiment of parachute infantry, but this was the basic structure.

While I was learning how to fall out of airplanes and blow things up, the guys already in the division were doing it for real. The 82nd took part in the invasion of Sicily in July 1943. Spearheading that attack was the 505th Regimental Combat Team—my future brothers in arms.

It was the first time a regiment-sized airborne attack had been tried by America, and it didn't go exactly as planned. High winds and poor navigation conspired to send the paratroopers wildly off course and hopelessly spread out; many of the first night's objectives could not be achieved. Worse, a planned drop on the second night of the operation by elements of the 504th Regiment was devastated by friendly fire. As the planes carrying the paratroopers flew over Allied ships offshore, gunners mistook them for enemy bombers. Twenty-three transports went down; eighty-one men died, including Brigadier General Charles Keerans, who was the division's assistant commander.

Despite all this, the 82nd's paratroopers played an important role in the early stages of the Sicily campaign. Scattered inland farther than intended, they grouped into small units and harassed German and Italian forces attempting to rush against the invaders. This allowed the American troops in the seaborne invasion to gain a better foothold and move farther inland. The ability to improvise and fight in small groups would remain a trademark of airborne soldiers for the rest of the war.

The 505th had jumped in a few minutes ahead of schedule on Sicily, earning itself the nickname "H-minus"; being early to battle was a badge of honor and became the unit motto. (H Hour is the hour of a planned attack; it does for "Hour" what "D Day" does for the date. At the time of the Sicily invasion, D-Day was still a general term for the launch of an assault; it wasn't until June 1944 that it became something much more.)

The 505th jumped into Paestum, Italy, in September 1943, helping the American forces that had attacked nearby Salerno. Far more accurate than the jump on Sicily, the operation's success was at least partly due to the use of newly created Pathfinder companies. These soldiers would jump ahead of the main airborne units, guiding those who followed to the proper DZs, or drop zones. The accurate jump allowed the 505th to act as a more coherent force, engaging the Germans who had counterattacked the invasion force and relieving pressure on the American troops who'd landed by sea.

The 82nd Airborne continued to fight in Italy, entering Naples on October 1. The 82nd's 504th Parachute Infantry Regiment took part in the bloody Anzio landings; instead of landing by parachute, they were brought in by sea in landing craft. Though they fought bravely, the Anzio campaign was a fiasco; the paratroopers were forced to dig foxholes and fight on the defensive rather than being used as offensive force multipliers. The 504th remained in the battle for roughly two months, fighting so ferociously that one German officer called them "Devils in Baggy Pants"—a nickname the unit adopted as its own after finding his diary after a battle.

The 82nd pulled out of Italy and northern Africa in early 1944, traveling to bases in Great Britain to prepare for the invasion of France. That was where I joined them, a replacement for men who had been killed in those earlier battles.

The veterans treated me and the other newcomers well, but there was a bit of distance between us and them. The tight binds that combat forms between fighters—the danger and emotion that welds them into a "band of brothers"—hadn't wrapped us in yet. I would imagine that there was also a bit of reluctance to make friendships too quickly. These guys already knew what war was about, how close ties can be severed in a half breath.

ROMAN CANDLES

What we knew about war was still theoretical: the parts that could be taught by maneuvers and training.

We trained a few weeks in Ireland and then moved on to England near Nottingham, where we'd spend time in a number of bases, though always in the same general area.

There weren't enough tents for us at first, and I lived with a family for about a week. They seemed pretty happy to have us. I gave the kids the candy bars I had; that might have helped. The English didn't have much to eat, and anything sweet was a real luxury.

I thought I'd been pretty well prepared in the States, but these maneuvers took things a lot further. There were live-fire exercises, where you'd be shot at. It was said that the gunfire was well over our heads, designed to get us used to the sound of combat without actually doing us harm. But a lot of those rounds *felt* close.

The most important thing I learned—though I didn't realize it at the time—was how to operate German weapons. We were given their handguns, rifles, grenades, and a neat little antitank weapon called the Panzerfaust. I learned to use them all.

Functionally, the Panzerfaust was similar to our bazooka. It fired a projectile meant to penetrate a tank. A recoilless rifle—to use the technical term—was basically a long tube with a simple sighting mechanism near the front. It fired a cone-shaped charge—it looked like a small cone stuck fat-end into the fat-end of another cone; the pointy end hit the target, penetrating and exploding. Folded fins spun out as the bullet was launched, stabilizing its flight. Once loaded, shooting the weapon was relatively simple; there was a lever directly behind the sight; press down and *waa-huush*—the shell flew at the target.

Like our bazooka—which fired differently—the weapon didn't pack enough punch to take out a main battle tank head-on. But its shaped charge could penetrate weak spots, like those at the back of the tank. And the charges were effective against "softer" vehicles like trucks and even light-armored personnel carriers such as the half-tracks the Germans liked. You could even punch a good hole in a building with one.

Knowing how to use the enemy's weapons was important because we expected to be fighting behind the lines, maybe for an extended period of time. We couldn't be sure of resupply, and could only carry so much ammo. I for one was sure I could put any

German weapon to much better use than its original intention—
firing at them, rather than me.

———————

Jumping from airplanes really agreed with me, and I found a way
to "practice" even when the unit had no scheduled exercises. Since
we were usually quartered on an air base, we were pretty close to
the areas where mechanics would repair bombers and transports
that had been shot up during missions over Europe. These aircraft
always needed to be given a check flight after being repaired. I
discovered that the aircrews often didn't mind if you tagged along
to take a jump.

The pilots were very accommodating, and would even
plan their flight path so you could jump close enough to the
barracks that it wasn't too difficult to get back . . . but not close
enough to be sliced into pieces by an errant plane on the runway.

When I had off time, I would head to our hangar, pack a chute—
learning to set up your own was part of our early training—and
then find a willing crew. I'd go back to the bomb bay, wait until
we reached altitude and position, then: bombs away.

These practice jumps were done with my reserve chute, which
was smaller than the regular T-5, but could be pulled by a rip cord
at the front. Between the chute and the altitude, everything happened a little faster than on a "normal" jump—but that was a plus
as far as I was concerned. I was still having a blast falling from
the sky.

All parachutes at the time were nothing like modern gear, and
were a far cry from the squarish T-11, which as we're writing this
is the standard parachute used by army paratroopers. Ours had

round canopies and were difficult to steer, whole different beasts than the sports chutes common today. But they were steerable, and with a bit of practice and some luck you could get pretty close to where you wanted.

Canvas straps connected to the lines running up to the chute. Pulling on these front risers turned you left or right, responding to the pull—down right, you moved right; left, you went left. Pulling on both at the same time made you move toward the ground faster, giving you some control forward and back.

Of course, it was important to jump at the right spot to begin with. That would be signaled by the pilot, with the final check by the jumpmaster. Your starting altitude also made a difference; more height might give you more time to maneuver, but it could also give the wind more time to interfere with your course—not to mention more time for anyone on the ground to take a shot at you.

I had more fun on the weekends than I would have had traveling to London or one of the towns closer to where we were quartered. I wasn't much of a partier; I didn't care to drink much beer, let alone the harder stuff. I couldn't see wasting the money going to town only to have a headache the next day. And I was very careful about my money, a lesson I'd learned from the Depression.

Jumping—or more accurately falling, if we're talking about going out from a bomb bay—from a plane isn't without its dangers and adventures. One time on a jump from a C-47 with my team, my chute managed to get itself tangled around the static line as it deployed. We called this a Roman candle—you spun and fell fast. Fortunately, my reserve opened fine when I pulled the cord. I landed a little fast but without getting hurt. Another time, two of the cells in the canopy collapsed, causing me to come down harder than I liked. Still, it wasn't so hard that I didn't go back for more.

Did I ever get used to jumping out of planes?

Heck, no.

That was the fun of it. Every time was as exciting as the first.

Of course, you do remember some jumps mostly for what happens afterward. We were on a maneuver over the English midlands, near Leicester and Nottinghamshire, when I went out. It was a pleasant English afternoon, but for some reason the wind currents insisted on carrying me away from the intended landing point; I stopped into a large yard with my commander, who'd gone out around the same time.

We were gathering our chutes and preparing for a long hike back when a group of nuns hailed us from a nearby building. We'd landed on the property of a convent. Before we could apologize, the ladies invited us inside for some tea and cookies.

You can't refuse an offer like that, especially in wartime.

The only jumps I hated were night jumps. It wasn't the falling I minded; it was the landing. Jumping at night meant you couldn't see the ground—or anything between you and the ground, like the tree I landed in the first and only time I did a night jump in England.

I got scratched up pretty bad. That was better than breaking my leg or my neck, but I worried about what would happen if I had to jump at night in combat. Land in a tree and even conscious I would be a sitting duck, maybe even helpless. Getting out of a parachute harness is one thing; getting out of it in the dark when you're hanging from a tree and weighed down by all your equipment is quite another. Simply jumping down may be the best option—but that's hard to gauge in the dark.

LETTER HOME

The night jump in England was one signal that we were getting closer to the invasion. I'd known since I left the States that attacking France was our goal—or at least I hoped it was our goal. I wanted to see action—all this practice had to mean something, and kicking the Germans out of France would mean a lot.

Our practice assignments became a lot more specific. We were tasked with blowing up bridges, very specific kinds of bridges, and we kept at it. It wasn't exactly hard to figure out that our job was probably going to involve something like that.

But when?

As the weather warmed, so did my anticipation. I have to admit that I enjoyed the exercises, especially the ones pitting, say, one company against another. The company commander would lay out a plan and we'd be off, generally for a day and a half; we would tackle a problem that included small-group infantry and engineering tactics all in one.

That sounds too technical.

We would be assigned to blow up a bridge. Another company would try and stop us.

Surprise attack at night. But they're expecting that. Hit the enemy where and when they least expect it. Can you get under the bridge and set the charges without them knowing? Maybe a diversion will get them off guard at Point A while you attack or sneak into Point B. Maybe a brute force attack makes sense . . .

And so on.

As an engineer specialist, I was assigned to a number of different companies and patrols; I even worked with different regiments. It got me used to working with a variety of people; I learned that teamwork doesn't depend on you having a long-standing relationship with someone, or even being a friend. The objective is the important thing.

I don't remember much about most of the men I was working with then; they've faded beyond very hazy blurs; I can't even call up most of their names.

First Sergeant Jim McKinsey. There's an exception.

McKinsey—I hope I have his name right after all these years—was a real stiff guy for regulations. He wanted you to be very well ordered—what the present-day soldiers call "squared away." Your uniform had to be just so. You didn't just march, you marched with gusto.

Sometimes, that kind of sharp discipline can be a bit much. But let me say this for my first sergeant: he was an all-around good soldier. I think his attitude in England was along the lines of: *Let me have these guys toe the line here, so they'll be sharp in France.*

And it worked. We had some very good sergeants—noncommissioned officers or non-coms, as we called them. Non-com leadership is critical for paratroopers. McKinsey had been in the Civilian Conservation Corps before the war—something he credited with shaping him as a leader—but a good number of our sergeants had been in the regular Army. So they had a head start not only on the Army's ways, but on discipline, tactics, and most of all, leadership.

Not to get ahead of myself, but McKinsey was one of the first killed when we hit Normandy. You could say that for a lot of my stick.

I didn't witness most of those deaths, but the memory of loss remains after all these years, even as the names have faded.

———————

I was writing letters home to Arlene and my family as often as possible, squeezing my sentences across the thin paper, trying not to compromise readability for space. At the same time, I couldn't say much about the war and what we were up to. Censors went through all the mail, and would cut out anything that might hint at strategy or tactics if it fell into enemy hands.

Mundane daily life was the only thing I could mention, and even then I had to be vague. But I felt like I needed to keep up the connection home, and that meant writing letters.

May 19, 1944

Dearest Mom & Dad

I know it is about time for me to write because I haven't written to you for almost six days but I have been awful busy. I received three letters from you this week and I sure was glad to get them. I am really terribly sorry to hear about little Larry dying; he was such a nice little fellow. I know that Clark boy that was killed. I believe he was the one that went to school with Ray and he was really a swell fellow. I'm glad to hear that we have a nice garden at home. Tell dad to take it easy and not to work too hard. Thanks a million for the candy you are sending but you really should save the money because you can use it in a better way; it won't hurt me to forget candy for a while but when I come home I will really make up for it. But it will really taste good now. How is Ed doing at work and tell him to keep saving his money. He will soon have much more than I have. How is Elena doing? Tell all of the kids "hello" for me and to write soon. How is Dorothy and Roy Jr.? Fine I hope. Boy, I really wish I could be there and have some of that cream pie you were talking about.

I received a letter from LeRoy the other day. He can't get away from his place either. But we are going to try to arrange a place for us to meet halfway between our camps "if" I can even get a twenty-four hour pass. Have you gotten that $80 I sent to you? I hope you get it soon; otherwise, I'll tell the company clerk about it. Glad to hear old Silver is still all right. It soon will be fun to take him hunting again. I never knew that Bob Simmons was over here. I would like to see him, too. You said not to get mad because you sent the candy. You know I would never get mad because I like the candy a lot. But you should really have saved the money instead of spending it on me. Glad to hear that all the folks back home will be behind us when the trouble starts over here. The sun has been shining here all the time. Boy, guess I am getting a bad case of spring fever because the weather has been really nice.

Well I guess I had better get on the ball and finish this letter as bad as it is, hahaha. By the way, Mom, how is the weather back in good old Iowa? I'm really glad to hear dad is making such good money. I bet I'll not know the house when I get back. Well, Mom, my letter will be getting too heavy for air mail so I must close. Take good care of yourselves and be good, hahaha.

Your loving son
Henry

(Larry was a neighbor boy who'd been hit by a car; Roy was my brother LeRoy, whom we usually called Roy in the family. Dorothy and Roy Jr. were his wife and child. Elena is my sister. And Bob Simmons—honestly, I don't remember him, but he must have been a neighbor.)

———————————

I had arranged for the Army to send a portion of my pay directly to my parents, and would send extra money every so often.

I'm not sure whatever became of the cash that I'd sent that's mentioned in that letter. Theft among soldiers was not unheard-of, though I'd rather not believe that anyone in my unit had sticky fingers.

Every community in America was touched by the war in many ways. The deaths my mom had told me about were just the tip of the iceberg. By the end of 1944, the Army had nearly eight million men in uniform, along with some 150,000 women, who served in the Women's Army Corps, more commonly known as WACs. Another three million men were in the Navy, with about a hundred thousand women in that force's auxiliary, known as WAVES—Women Accepted for Voluntary Emergency Service. There were another 475,000 men in the Marines and over 171,000 in the Coast Guard, which was not only patrolling the coastal waters but was supplying personnel and ships for more traditional Navy missions, including amphibious landings. Add in the Merchant Marine and people who were technically civilians like the WASPs (Women's Airforce Service Pilots) ferrying aircraft, and you have a picture of the country at war. The U.S. population in 1940 was counted at 132 million; about 43 percent were between the ages of eighteen and forty-five. Well over half the men in their prime were in uniform or doing something war related; the percentage was even higher for those in their twenties.

———————

I didn't get a chance to hook up with my brother—or any of the other neighbors serving in England. As May wound down, the sun kept shining, and we kept training. Officially, I did a little over thirty jumps through the end of the month—not a bad number for a new guy in the outfit. Unofficially, I had over sixty, thanks mostly to the aircrews that allowed me to hitchhike into the clouds and walk home.

Did all that jumping help?

I think so. The more you do something, the better you get at it. I became comfortable with the weight and feel of my equipment, and confident that I could handle an emergency.

But mostly it was fun. I just loved jumping.

———————

Far above my pay grade, the generals and their staffs were making decisions about where and how to invade, what forces to move when, and all the other details that a successful invasion would rely on.

I had about as much to do with those decisions as a piece of paper can decide on the way the wind will blow. I did get close to two of the top decision makers, though—General Dwight D. Eisenhower and British prime minister Winston Churchill.

The VIPs came to inspect our unit while we were getting ready to make a jump. Eisenhower was the Allies' supreme commander for the invasion, the man coordinating the attack and its vast forces. Churchill had headed the British government since 1940, easily identified by even an Iowa kid as the single most important political leader in the alliance.

I was in the second row, close enough to reach out and grab the prime minister's cigar.

No shenanigans. I stood at strict attention the whole time.

Churchill had his bulldog with him. I swear, the dog looked just like him.

Everything about Eisenhower screamed leader, his bearing, the look in his eyes. He was in a jovial mood that day, and stopped often to talk to the men in the front row. It happened that a trooper from Kansas was standing right in front of me.

"I understand you're from my state," Ike said to him.

"Yes, sir," replied the private.

"They feeding you good?"

"Yes, sir."

Eisenhower nodded and moved on.

That was as close as I got to the top man in the war.

On May 27, I sat down to write another letter to my parents. By now we knew that we were going into France very soon, though we still hadn't been given the exact details. I started and stopped the letter over the next several days, writing between drills and taking care of other business.

May 27, 1944

Dearest Mom & Dad:

I'm sorry this is the first chance I have had to write this week. I have been pretty busy. I have quite a bit of washing to do tomorrow so I shall be busy most of the day. Sunday is a workday here as well as any place else.

Say, Mom, I meant to ask you in [your] other letter whether you have received my $80 or not. I sent it about two or three weeks ago. So write and let me know if you received it, please.

How is dad coming along with the garden and how is our garden? Everything must be well on the way of growing because it is almost June now. They will be having summer vacations at home next week, won't they?

I'll bet all the kids will really like that.

I know I always looked forward to summer vacation.

Today is Sunday and the weather here is really fine. It could not be better.

How are Dorothy and Roy Jr.? He must be a pretty big fellow by now. I'll bet LeRoy sure would like to see him and it probably won't be long before he does. I just finished my washing a few moments ago. I always have to wash on Sunday because that is the only time I have time enough. We are going to have chicken for dinner today. That's something that is rather rare over here. I still haven't had a chance to see LeRoy yet but I hope to very soon.

I have been on this letter two days so far. I finished one page yesterday and writing the rest on Sunday. I'm sorry I have to use such large envelopes but they are the only ones I have. I [am] saving coins now, some from Sicily, Italy, France, and England and some good old American money for luck.

Well, mother, time is getting short so I must close now but I shall write you again soon.

Your loving son
Henry.

It was the last letter they'd get from me: Not long after finally finishing it, I was told to grab my gear and board a truck for a new base. There was something in the tone of our officers and NCOs that we weren't going on another maneuver; the next time we jumped we would be landing in France.

THREE

June 1944

AT HOME

Looking back seventy-five years, the end of the war seems guaranteed by the spring of 1944. Russia had gone on the offensive east of Germany, beginning to take back territory it had lost in the German blitzkrieg of 1941. Fighting in Ukraine and Crimea, the Red Army battered the Germans. They took great losses of their own, but their bigger population and ability to supply their army from factories beyond German reach gave them unstoppable momentum.

In Italy, American troops were breaking free of Anzio, pushing the Germans farther north in heavy fighting.

In the Pacific, Allied forces were fighting the Japanese in Burma, and the United States was staging for an attack on Saipan in the Mariana Islands, an offensive that would lead to air bases within range of the Japanese mainland.

American and British bombers were flying around the clock, striking tactical targets in France as well as strategic ones in Germany. Anything that might help the Germans respond to an invasion was bombed, then bombed again. Meanwhile, the villages and towns of southern England were overflowing with troops waiting to take part in that invasion.

But on the ground at that moment, with those troops back in the States, there was no sense of inevitable victory. We were confident we would win, but we had no way of knowing when the ultimate victory would come. And we didn't know the cost. Our leaders had agreed that they would accept only unconditional surrender, and surely that meant there would be ferocious fighting ahead.

Back home, Franklin Delano Roosevelt had run for a third term as president in 1940, breaking the historical precedent set by George Washington that a president would only serve two terms. Roosevelt had named Secretary of Agriculture Henry Wallace to run as his vice president, itself a controversial decision because he had been a Republican earlier. Despite the fact that Wallace was from Iowa, Roosevelt lost in my home state.

It was the reverse of 1932 and 1936, when he'd won easily. There were a lot of reasons for that loss in 1940. One was history—Republicans usually won in Iowa. And a lot of people didn't like the idea of a three-term president. But another was opposition to war, and a lot of people thought Roosevelt was more likely than his opponent, Wendell Willkie, to get us involved.

People forget that now. America didn't want war. We didn't want to be involved. Before Pearl Harbor, of course.

Willkie's argument that Roosevelt would involve the United States in the European conflict found a lot of favor throughout the States, and not just in Republican areas like Iowa. Roosevelt won the election with about 55 percent of the popular vote and

449 electoral votes to Willkie's 82, but the results were not as big as the landslides he had enjoyed in 1932 and 1936.

Now, in 1944, he decided to run for a fourth term. Many in the Midwest, including Iowa, would oppose him for reasons that included the New Deal. There is a saying—*Don't change horses in midstream*. And a lot of others about staying with a winning hand. Those applied to the war, and the economy. But people were looking at other things, too, and while Roosevelt would win, his totals were the lowest of his four elections.

Roosevelt was my commander-in-chief, but I couldn't vote for him. Or against him, for that matter: the voting age back then was still twenty-one. I could die for my commander, but not vote for him.

Well, and I guess the truthful thing to say is that, being nineteen, I wasn't much keyed into politics.

The war was important to people. But it wasn't the only thing they thought about.

Economically, though, the United States was all in. War mode ruled. Factories ran night and day. My little city of Clinton had not quite returned to its lumber glory days, but the factories were doing well and there was plenty of work all around. My father had found a good-paying job at the railroad as a car maintainer; he would hold that job until he died years later.

Arlene was working in a local factory making the stands for machine guns. She'd gotten her mother a position there, too. They would work a twelve-hour night shift, coming home in time to get the younger boys off to school, handle the laundry, and cook some food for Arlene's dad and the kids. A little rest, and they'd be back at it again. Sometimes seven days a week. It was a half mile to work; they walked it every day.

The money was one reason they worked, of course. But along-side of that, they felt good about helping the war effort. A lot of people, women especially, felt exactly the same. Maybe they couldn't be on the front lines with us, but they could at least do something.

The feeling wasn't unanimous, though, and not everyone wanted to fight. The draft continued; many of our younger brothers and friends were in the military or would soon be drafted. Even so, the Army feared a manpower shortage. Part of this had to do with organization—having the right sort of fighting men doing the right sort of things, like manning antiaircraft units or armor. Projections made at the beginning of the war could become obsolete while a new division was still in training—or worse, had just taken the field. It took time to reorganize divisions and train men to do different tasks, let alone to equip them. And the introduction of a new weapon could set off a whole chain of reorganization; a new bomber meant new pilots and crew, possibly new airfields and new procedures. Projections on the number of infantrymen needed in Europe were especially low, and a whole range of adjustments were needed to fix this.

But the manpower shortage was also due to shortfalls in volunteers and the draft. Besides deferments for men doing work critical to national defense, the Selective Service was originally reluctant to draft men with young children. This changed as the war went on, until 1944, when about half of the men who had young families were being selected.

People thought about the war. Most were very patriotic. But the war was neither won nor the only thing on their minds every minute of every day.

OVERLORD

The plans to invade France, code-named Overlord, went through many variations before they were finalized in mid-May. But there were always some common features: a large-scale landing by multiple armies, with the bulk of the fighting to be done by American, British, and Canadian troops. It would be launched with complete control of the sea and the air, and would follow a concerted effort to soften defenses inland as well as on the beaches.

Once Normandy was chosen for the landing, the general shape of the assault was set. An area of fifty miles was selected for the seaborne assault, stretching from Colleville-sur-Orne west of Caen Canal to the area in front of St.-Martin-de-Varreville on the Cotentin Peninsula. The assault was divided into two forces. The eastern half, with British and Canadian soldiers, would land on three beaches code-named Sword (north of Caen), Juno (north of Ver-sur-Mer), and Gold (near Arromanches).

The western force was striking two areas much farther apart: Omaha, which extended roughly from Sainte-Honorine-des-Pertes to west of Vierville-sur-Mer, and Utah, on the Cotentin Peninsula, west of the Douve and Vire Rivers. The forces were American; VII Corps with men drawn from the 4th Infantry, 90th Infantry, and 4th Cavalry on Utah, and V Corps, with the 1st Infantry Division and the as-yet-untested 29th Infantry. A small force of Rangers was tasked for a key (and later famous) mission against gun emplacements at the western end of Omaha, known to us as Point-du-Hoc.

The American beaches were pretty far apart, which would leave them vulnerable to counterattack on the flanks. Utah was also considered a difficult area to hold against counterattack because there were limited ways for the forces to exit the beachhead. If an enemy quickly responded to these assaults, the landings there could fail. And the failure of one, especially Omaha, would endanger the others. It was not hard for the planners to envision a nightmare scenario with German troops and tanks rolling across the countryside, down to the beaches, flattening everything in sight.

Which was where we came in.

The very first invasion plans had a tiny role for airborne troops—and none for the 82nd. By the beginning of May, we were a critical part. The 82nd Airborne and our sister 101st Airborne Division were tasked with landing ahead of the sea invasion and cutting off the main German routes to the Utah Beach area. After that was accomplished, we would assist in slicing the entire Cotentin Peninsula off from further reinforcement. That would mean that the port at the northern end of the peninsula, Cherbourg, could be easily attacked and taken. Cherbourg could then be used to funnel supplies to the armies. The peninsula would also provide a route for Patton's Third Army to sweep westward toward the French coast when it landed later.

That broad-stroke outline translated into a series of very specific actions planned in greater and greater detail as the plan was passed on down the chain of command, from the army group to the army level, to the corps level, to the division level, to the regiment and so on until it reached our company and the "stick" or subgroup that would jump together in the first phase of the battle.

The 82nd Airborne's overall operation was called Mission Boston. About 370 C-47s would transport 6,420 troopers to the Cotentin Peninsula of France, dropping us in an area a little more than an hour's march from Utah Beach. Roughly five miles wide, the targeted landing area was between Valagnes and Carentan, in the vicinity of Sainte-Mère-Église. As part of the plan to achieve tactical surprise and lessen casualties, the C-47s would leave England at low altitude—five hundred feet—skim over the English Channel, and make landfall before rising to about 1,500 for the drop. This would make it hard for German radar to "see" the planes. It would also make the drop relatively low and fast—less time to get shot at, though a bit harder on the legs.

Three regiment combat teams would take part, with three distinct drop zones; in each case Pathfinders who had hit the ground some thirty minutes before would help guide the planes in. The three RCTs were mine, the 505th, and the 507th and 508th. Only the 505th had seen combat before; because of this, its companies were assigned the toughest missions. The 325th Infantry Glider Regiment and some more support units were set to arrive on June 7 with additional men and supplies.

The 505th's targets were close to Sainte-Mère-Église, the most important objective of the night—which is not to say that any of the other missions were superfluous. A decent-sized village that sat about five miles west of the Utah beaches, Sainte-Mère-Église had a small contingent of German forces, but its value was its proximity to some of the easy routes to Utah. Route N13 ran straight through the village's business area; it could easily be used to bring troops into the area and surrounding countryside. There was also a nearby train line, which potentially might be used despite the severe attacks on German rail in the lead-up to the battle.

The problem for the Germans using that route on D-Day, though, would be to get from Sainte-Mère-Église eastward to where our guys were coming off the landing craft. While there were a few nearby roads heading in that direction, they had a common problem: if you started from Sainte-Mère-Église, you had to cross the Merderet River.

Which meant using a bridge.

That's where I came in.

Some area bridges were to be blown up; others looked useful for our future operations. The specifics on what to do with each varied. Ideally, the men from the 505th Regimental Combat Team assigned to land near the village would take control and capture the bridges nearby. Ideally, these bridges would be kept intact, and used by our forces at some point after the initial landing.

But if this couldn't happen—if the Germans mounted such a massive counterattack that we were overwhelmed and they regained or held the bridges, then the job would be to blow them up.

My bridge was at Chef-du-Pont, about a mile and a half south of Sainte-Mère-Église. It was a tiny bridge—almost a culvert over a narrow creek outside of the hamlet. The Germans had flooded the area, making the area look like a lake. The bridge and its causeway were the only raised land, and the only way across the bending river in that area.

Six of us combat engineers were selected to work with "regular" paratroopers assigned to Chef-du-Pont. I was the lone engineer in a stick that would be dropped in an area to the west of Sainte-Mère-Église. We were to hook up after the jump and work together on our objective. That would mean get on the ground, find the rest of the unit if possible, and move to the bridge.

Why was I chosen?

I could sooner tell you who will win next week's lottery than give you a correct answer. Maybe they thought I was good at blowing up bridges. Maybe they thought I wasn't good at blowing up bridges, and put me in with a lot of other fellows who were. Maybe a million other reasons—your guess is as good as mine.

As I recall, I had never met any of the engineers I was supposed to work with. I'd spent my time in England working directly with 505 platoons from the beginning; whether these men had done the same or stayed with the 307th's companies I have no idea. I think they'd arrived in England after me, but I didn't get much chance to talk to them on the plane.

In fact, I really didn't know the rest of the soldiers on the stick. I'd worked with a couple, but not long enough to form close friendships with any of them.

Names . . .

I remember *John Blanchard,* a private. Nice guy.

Bryant. Cheerful, young. Liked to go to town and have a bit of fun.

Lieutenant Kaddish.

Or Caddish.

Howard . . .

I've always been terrible with names, and now the years have made it even worse. Memory is a fleeting thing.

Not knowing the men wasn't a handicap. I trusted that we were all going to do our jobs well. They were fellow paratroopers, so automatically they were brothers.

That's the way I thought. That's the way we all thought.

Let me sketch out a little more of Overlord, starting with the airborne troops. Sainte-Mère-Église and the Merderet River were hardly the only strategic spots inland that needed to be secured that night. The 101st Airborne division would land generally south and east of the 82nd's drops. They were charged with controlling the exits from the Utah beaches as well as watching the Douve River. Their flights were due to take off about thirty minutes ahead of ours, with the same low-altitude tactics to avoid radar. Like us, they would be guided by Pathfinders' beacons, hopefully increasing the accuracy of the jumps and allowing for the men to join together and fight as larger units.

On the eastern end of the Overlord assault, British paratroopers in the 6th Airborne Division would land near the city of Caen, targeting German artillery at the mouth of the Orne River as well as cutting off or delaying a counterattack.

Caen was a major priority not just for the British troops landing at Juno, but for the entire operation. Once secured—something British commanding general Bernard Montgomery optimistically thought could be accomplished by the end of the first day—Allied troops would swing eastward, striking across northern France.

Approximately 9,500 aircraft would support Overlord; the number included 832 C-47 Dakotas, our buses to the battlefield. Two hundred ships would train their guns on the shore; the number of transports and landing craft was almost too high to count. There were over four thousand landing craft of different sizes and configuration; many were Higgins boats, rectangular-shaped, flat-hulled boats that today are most commonly associated with assault.

Onshore, the French Resistance had received secret orders to harass German assets. Their campaign had begun days before with attacks against railways and proceeded to electrical stations and finally barracks and depots. Telephone lines were to be cut the night we jumped in. These guerrilla attacks had a twofold value:

German soldiers who might have responded to D-Day were killed or deprived of ammunition and the means of transportation and communication. And the attacks tied down a number of German units as they sought to catch the Resistance and prevent fresh ambushes.

More than 150,000 men were going to land in the invasion; roughly half were American. Some 34,000 were headed for Omaha Beach; another 23,000 were intended for Utah. Our parachute assault would be the largest Allied airborne assault of the war, with roughly 15,000 from the 82nd and 101st.

That was just the first day; other troops would be coming in on Day Two . . . and Three, Four, and so on, until a massive, overwhelming force was present.

THE GERMANS

A large force was needed, given that the Germans had a big one waiting for the attack.

The Germans had fifty divisions in France and the nearby Netherlands and Belgium. An entire Panzer Corps had been transferred out of the country to help with the battles on the Eastern Front with Russia, and many of the units in France were either short on manpower or still trying to recover after being rotated out of the East. But the Germans still had a sizable force of Panzer tanks and grenadiers available to strike at the landing.

The main force on the peninsula across from the troops landing at Utah was the 709th Static Infantry Division. "Static" divisions were units primarily organized for occupation and defense. The division troops included former USSR prisoners of war who had volunteered to fight for the Germans rather than being imprisoned.

These defensive-minded units were not equipped with the large number of vehicles required for modern offenses, and most military planners regarded them as a notch—or several notches—below frontline troops. Their quality varied widely, but given a prepared position, plenty of weapons, and adequate leadership, they could do a good job on defense. The 709th had spent several months in the area preparing defenses and knew the terrain almost as well as the natives.

An even tougher and more mobile unit had moved into the area in May—the German 91st Airlanding Division—what we would call "air mobile" today, minus the helicopters. They were trained and equipped to move via air, and were considered among the elite infantry units in Normandy. Intelligence reports of the division's movements got a lot of attention at headquarters, changing the plans for our landings at the last minute. The 82nd's drop zones were moved closer together, shifted nearer to the 101st. I never knew about those changes, of course, and they wouldn't have made any difference to me if I had. My job was to go when the green light came on, and one bridge would have been more or less the same.

————————

While we didn't know it, conflict between Oberbefehlshaber West (Supreme Commander West) Field Marshal Gerd von Rundstedt and Army Group B commander Field Marshal Erwin Rommel hamstrung the Germans when the time would come to respond to the attacks.

Rommel is more famous to us as the Desert Fox who led German troops in Africa; Rundstedt had led large army groups against both France and the Soviet Union. Rundstedt was Rommel's boss, but Rommel's reputation and status as a favorite of Hitler gave him considerable influence and power. That made for an important conflict in the German plans and response to the invasion—which helped us unwittingly on D-Day.

Rommel, who was in charge of the defenses, had preached a philosophy of stopping the invasion on the beaches; part of that strategy was to add thousands of fortifications, booby traps, and mines to the beach area.

His philosophy also called for quick counterstrikes from areas nearby, aiming to literally push the Allies back into the water. Rundstedt favored a more centralized approach, with a larger counterstrike once we were onshore. What ended up happening was largely a bad compromise between the two. And the disagreements between the two generals didn't help communication among the staffs during battle.

The Germans were also hurt by elaborate Allied disinformation campaigns and counterintelligence aimed at convincing them that the attack was aimed elsewhere. The most successful—and famous—had George Patton at the head of an army that would strike in the area of the port of Calais, far north of the actual beaches. Calais made sense for many reasons—the distance across the English Channel was short, and Calais would present the Allies with an excellent port to resupply troops through. Patton was a famous general, and it was natural that he would lead such an invasion—and in fact, he'd been considered when Bradley was chosen instead. The operation was so successful that even on D-Day, the Germans weren't sure at first whether it was a diversion, meant to take their attention away from Calais.

FALSE START

At the very end of May we were taken to quarantine—a barbed-wire camp at Spanhoe Airfield, in Northamptonshire, England, about eighty miles north of London. Not only were we behind the wire, but armed MPs patrolled the area. They were as much to keep us in as keep spies out. We weren't allowed to talk to anyone—including the MPs.

The commanders started going over the plan with us using sand tables, three-dimensional mock-ups that gave you a rough idea of the elevation and layout. Key features were prominent—one of the important ones was the church and village of Sainte-Mère-Église. The church spire was the sort of landmark you could use to orient yourself even from a few miles away; I quickly memorized it.

The town of Sainte-Mère-Église had existed for hundreds of years, centered on a church nearly as old. The houses clustered in a cross, almost an X if you looked at it from the right angle. The place had known plenty of blood in its long history, having been a focal point during the Hundreds Years' War.

Not one of the briefers mentioned that history. Even if they knew it, I'm sure none of us who would be parachuting there would have cared. We were more interested in how the city might be defended, and the fields nearby, which seemed to promise easy landings.

Not easy, but manageable.

Three drop areas were designated, with the village roughly in the middle. Each unit had a different task, from taking control of the town to getting a hold of the bridges. Talking among ourselves, some of the veterans thought the plan was good, and that we'd have an easy time—if we were not spread out when we jumped.

On June 3, we got the word: We'd board our planes late the next day and jump into Normandy after 0001 June 5. Once again, everything was laid out on the sand tables. At the last minute, I was tasked to work with an infantry unit from the 505's Company F, one of the units assigned to capture the bridge at Chef-du-Pont.

I was ready. My job was simple: help capture the bridge. And if the men I was with couldn't do that, I'd blow it up.

Easy.

———————

Briefing done, we went back to what we'd been doing. New equipment was issued, including a pocket-sized Bible.

I wasn't much on religion, but I thought, why not take it? It's free.

I read it as history, and I read quite a bit over the next few days. There wasn't that much else to do, really. I wrote letters to my mother and Arlene that would be sent after the invasion. I checked and rechecked my gear. Other guys cleaned their weapons for the umpteenth time. There were card games and dice—there were always card games and dice. A few guys read books or comics or whatever they had. Still more just waited.

And waited.

Church services were offered that night. I wasn't a real believer—closer, I think to an atheist, even if they say there are none in war. But I went to the service anyway. Maybe I sensed there was something more to life than I'd known until then. Maybe I was just bored.

———————

One thing the minister said stays with me today: *You're fighting for what is right.*

———————

On D-Day, paratroopers generally carried some seventy pounds of gear into combat; because of my equipment as a combat engineer, I carried a bit more, not only in my ruck and other gear on my body, but in a satchel attached to my leg.

What did I have?

There was the main chute, of course, along with a reserve. My Thompson submachine gun and eight magazines—we usually called them clips, though that's not technically correct—of ammo, with each mag holding thirty rounds. I also had five mags for my .45. I had a long rope I could use for climbing out of trees or off a building if I got stuck landing. Then there was my trench knife, whose handle was molded as brass knuckles. I carried a gas mask—we weren't sure if the Germans might use gas against us. A trenching tool—picture a short-handled, folding shovel. Compass. Flashlight.

K rations. Can't forget those. About three days' worth.

D-Bars—not-so-sweet-tasting chocolate bars for energy on the run.

Two concussion grenades. Four fragmentation grenades. Canteen, first aid packet. Pocket knife. Sulfur bandage. Toothbrush. Razor. Soap. Foot powder. Small oil can to clean my weapons.

I also had a fighting knife in my boot, just in case.

No change of clothes, aside from a pair of socks. And if there'd been room for anything else, it would have been ammo, not underwear.

I carried one other thing that most other paratroopers didn't: dynamite in the package that would be strapped to my leg when I jumped. There were fifteen or sixteen blocks of TNT, along with some Composition C (another explosive; think of it as a plastic explosive whose modern counterpart is C-4). I had four caps and some cord to set it all off. I also had a little plunger, just like you've seen in the movies.

TNT takes a bit to explode, as did Composition C. The caps were a different story. I carried them surrounded in cotton, and to the extent I could, kept them separated from the primer cord, and everything else for that matter.

Having spent much of my childhood living by railroad tracks where the rush of trains was my lullaby, I've always been able to sleep well no matter what else is going on around me. The night of June 3 was no exception. But when I got up, I found it was raining. The wind blew something fierce.

Bad sign.

We waited, but most of us probably knew—and maybe hoped—that the invasion would be put off because of the conditions. Our mission was critical to the invasion's success, and there was no way to jump in this weather. After all this preparation, we didn't want to miss the action.

Word soon came to stand down.

———————

These days they have computers, satellites, and fancy radar to predict the weather. Back then—let's just say meteorology was more art than absolute science.

At his secret headquarters in a trailer in Southwick, England, Eisenhower was faced with a huge dilemma. Not only was the weather for June 5 bad; the weathermen were concerned that it would remain that way through June 7 and maybe beyond.

Many factors had gone into the decision to set the invasion for June 5; among them were the position of the tides and depth of water at the beaches. That made for narrow slots when the attack could be launched. In this case, if the invasion didn't go off on June 6, it would have to be delayed at least two weeks.

Rescheduling the attack might have been an easy task a few months before, when the operation was still a matter of paper maps and thick reports. Now, though, there were 175,000 men aboard troopships or waiting nearby in ports. There were seven battleships in cruising distance of Normandy. There were a thousand things small and large that could tip the enemy off to our targets, giving him time to rush fresh troops to the area and meet our armies as they came off their boats.

So much had been set in motion that stopping it now was barely possible.

On the other hand, launching without proper air cover, without paratroopers behind the lines to cut off counterattacks, with the seas so high and wind so fierce that a good portion of the invasion force would drown before reaching the rocks and sands of Normandy—that, too, might spell disaster, not just for the operation but the war itself.

Eisenhower had been sorting through the problem since Friday, when the conflicting views among the meteorologists nonetheless pointed toward stormy conditions. "Full of menace" was the way the chief weatherman described the forecast.

The briefing got worse from there.

Eisenhower pressed the meteorologists for answers Saturday—would things clear up in time?

They could only guess, and guesses weren't good enough. Though ships had already sailed—and we were ready to go—the invasion was put off for twenty-four hours.

More card playing, more dice, more praying. Eisenhower spent a restless night. Forget the logistical nightmare and the potential loss of surprise—what would a delay do to morale?

———

There was one unexpected benefit to the bad weather. The Germans had forecasters, too, and they made the same dire predictions our guys had. Their conclusion was that the weather would remain poor. The high command relaxed. Rommel went home to Germany to celebrate his wife's birthday.

It was a slight moment of inattention. But those sorts of slips can mean everything in war.

THE SUN SMILES

———

I woke up June 5 to a full, smiling sun and a gentle breeze. I knew instantly this was going to be the day.

No. It didn't happen that way.

June 5 started out overcast and still a bit unpleasant. But I sensed that it was going to improve, and by the afternoon the sun *did* come out, and to a man we knew this was it. We didn't know about the intricacies of the tides or the tangled logistics already in motion; we just knew in our guts that we were finally going to get a chance to do the job we'd trained for over the past months.

You don't feel joy, exactly, when you're on the eve of a battle, or at least I didn't. It was more anticipation, a little bit of nerves, a lot of adrenaline. I thought a bit about home, my family, and Arlene.

Would I marry her?

Absolutely. She'd already said yes. I'd bought an engagement ring soon after arriving in England to seal the deal—though for some reason I couldn't find it now.

An omen?

More likely theft or maybe carelessness, or maybe it was somewhere at the bottom of the gear tucked away at the bottom of my barracks bag in the barracks.

Not likely.

I suspected a thief. Unfortunately, even an elite group like the 82nd had fellows with sticky fingers. We weren't all saints and heroes. Or maybe we were; it just depended on the circumstances. People can be thieves as well as heroes. You had to trust that the one next to you was more hero than thief on the battlefield.

There were other things to worry about that night: the location where we were jumping, the wind, the Germans. I'd never shot a man before.

I didn't worry too much about that. I checked my gear, my gun, and read my Bible. I used Arlene's photo as a bookmark, slowly turning the pages.

I joined the rest of my stick under the wing of our plane as the sun edged down. A few of us chatted about different things, none of them really important. Food. Girlfriends. Possible girlfriends.

A few didn't want to talk at all, keeping to themselves, probably thinking about some of the things I had.

Finally, we got the word and climbed aboard the C-47.

The big cargo planes had seats running along each side; depending on the version, they might be a straight bench or bucket seats—ours had the buckets. We were going in style.

You sat in the order you went out, usually one row standing and jumping, with the next side following. Ordinarily, the officer or a senior NCO in charge went out first, but that night I was next to the door: first up, first out. This wasn't an honor I got for being terrifically skilled, let alone for being the highest ranking or oldest on the plane. (The oldest man in my stick would have been around twenty-three; I may have been the youngest at nineteen, still a few months shy of my twentieth birthday.) I was gifted the position next to the door and first one out because I was carrying the explosives.

I think it was meant to give me the highest possibility of landing on target. Or maybe it was because the jumpmaster feared my bundle would trip someone or get tangled in the gear.

On the other hand, he may have been thinking that if we caught fire, it would be smart to get the explosives out first.

The door to the plane had been removed, and sitting next to it gave me a good view outside. I craned my neck around, watching as the aircraft's two engines came to life. We vibrated slowly across the field, joining a line of similar transports, each undoubtedly as overloaded as ours.

———————

Eisenhower visited some of the paratroop units before they took off. I don't recall seeing him, but I do remember his speech, which was to be broadcast or read to everyone taking part in the invasion. What stuck with me was the frank reality of his message: *Our enemy is well armed and prepared.*

Soldiers, Sailors, and Airmen of the Allied Expeditionary Force:

You are about to embark upon the Great Crusade, toward which we have striven these many months.

The eyes of the world are upon you. The hopes and prayers of liberty-loving people everywhere march with you.

In company with our brave Allies and brothers-in-arms on other Fronts you will bring about the destruction of the German war machine, the elimination of Nazi tyranny over oppressed peoples of Europe, and security for ourselves in a free world.

Your task will not be an easy one. Your enemy is well trained, well equipped, and battle-hardened. He will fight savagely.

But this is the year 1944. Much has happened since the Nazi triumphs of 1940–41. The United Nations have inflicted upon the Germans great defeats, in open battle, man-to-man. Our air offensive has seriously reduced their strength in the air and their capacity to wage war on the ground. Our Home Fronts have given us an overwhelming superiority in weapons and munitions of war, and placed at our disposal great reserves of trained fighting men. The tide has turned. The free men of the world are marching together to victory.

I have full confidence in your courage, devotion to duty, and skill in battle. We will accept nothing less than full victory.

Good Luck! And let us all beseech the blessing of Almighty God upon this great and noble undertaking.

Brigadier General James Gavin, the 82nd's second in command, gave his own speech:

Remember, you are going in to kill, or you will be killed.

We lumbered into the air. It was somewhere around two P.M., a little later. The Pathfinders were already en route, perhaps had even started to draw fire.

The plane rose slowly, then began to circle the field, waiting for the other planes to join up in the formation. Somewhere in the armada forming around us, Major General Matthew Ridgway, the 82nd commander, was aboard one of the lead planes, checking his gear, intending to jump with the first groups hitting France. His second in command, General Gavin, was in another aircraft. Airborne generals lead from the front.

I could see the moon out the door, and the outlines of other planes, many still rising, others flying in from one of the other airfields. France was out there somewhere, just an idea of a place, something I'd seen on a sand table, not real yet.

The guys near me talked about their girlfriends, whose was prettier.

Someone made a joke.

There was some laughter, more jokes.

We stopped circling. The moon shone bright in the sky. We may have been above the clouds, I may not have had much of an angle, I may just be misremembering after all of these years gone by, but I swear I could see a thousand ships on the English

Channel. I swear I can remember feeling a great deal of pride, knowing that my country had managed to produce all of these forces.

I swear I knew that with so many men, so many arms, surely victory lay ahead.

I glanced at a watch. We were less than a half hour from war, not thirty minutes from hell.

FOUR

Drop Zone

GREEN LIGHT

The immense armada all around us filled me with pride. I was part of a vast undertaking, a huge force mustered to free people who'd been imprisoned by the Nazis now for four years. I'd heard America called the Arsenal of Democracy; here was the evidence of that.

That grandiose sensation passed as we got closer to land. The sky had been clear when the plane dipped low to get in under the radar; now a bank of clouds appeared, cutting the light from above. Fog had rolled in over the land ahead.

Then something far more ominous appeared: flashes of light. Tracers. White nips of explosions in the air.

A red furl in the distance—fire. Another plane, probably, hit.

Then came the deluge. Not of rain, but of gunfire, big shells, small shells, every antiaircraft caliber imaginable. Not falling from the clouds but rising from the ground. The explosions buffeted the plane.

The Germans were on to us. Pathfinders had come in a short time earlier to mark the drop areas, and it's possible that their aircraft had alerted the defenses at the coast. It's just as likely that with so many planes flying so low to the ground, lookouts spotted us coming over the Channel and sounded the alarm. Guided by human vision or even primitive radar, antiaircraft fire can be notoriously inaccurate, but with hundreds of planes in the sky flying in a precise formation to hit very specific targets, the law of averages favor even the poorest gunner.

Whatever happened, we were under fire as we came over the French coast. Heavy fire.

In my mind's eye as I think back, I look again through the door, twisting around to see what was going on. I see a plane nearby catch fire and turn into a ball of flames. I see another with its wing tipping, diving quickly, inevitably toward the waves.

The seats on the C-47 weren't ever very comfortable, and with all the gear I feel pinched and cramped. I want to get going, get out of the plane—it is more dangerous, in my mind, to be sitting in a metal tube where I can't fight back than it would be on the ground.

We are over the Cotentin Peninsula, near Cherbourg, maybe past it, caught in a manic mash of gunfire.

The plane shakes. Shells or their shrapnel hit us.

Metal rips through our aircraft. It sounds like thousands of marbles falling on a thin piece of metal. A kind of metal tremble, an odd hail of rain.

The man next to me goes limp, collapsing down in his seat. He doesn't crumble; it's more like he was a kind of balloon, and suddenly deflates. The trooper on the bench across from me—I can't remember names now, no matter how hard I try—the same thing happens to him.

This is what death looks like. The first time I've seen it up close.

The plane hits a thick bank of fog. The engines roar. I smell burning metal.

The light to signal our jump is red. Get ready.

A green light flashes.

Green light! Jump!

Up! Go! Go! Go!

I latch on the cable, then push myself out the door as quickly as I can. We're going faster than normal, and we're lower than I thought—six hundred feet, five hundred. The gust off the engines smacks me. Gravity yanks me.

The pull from the prop wash as the chute fills . . .

The jerk on my leg as the satchel of explosives reaches the end of its tether . . .

I can't think. Every reaction is in slow motion.

My harness pulls tight, squeezing every part of my body. I pull the risers, trying in vain to steer.

On any other fall, there was an eerie quiet as I descended. Now there are noises—plane engines, gunfire, shouts . . .

Sainte-Mère-Église is below. There is a red glow. I'm falling into the village, not the field outside. There is nothing to do now but fall.

As best as I can remember and determine, the shrapnel that killed the two other paratroopers in my plane before I jumped came from a shell that hit the wing. I don't know what happened to our plane; at least one other aircraft near us exploded and crashed, but I think ours made it through and flew back to England.

Our flight had come in lower and faster than intended. I'm pretty sure the jump light came on too early. But once I was out, I was out.

Looking down, I realized I was falling into Sainte-Mère-Église, which I recognized from our briefings and the church in the center of town.

A church I could see very well, thanks to a fire in a building nearby. People were running all around, trying to put it out.

Others were looking upward.

Shooting.

The light of the fire must have silhouetted us against the sky. Not only was my targeted jump zone about a mile or two away, but a village filled with people shooting at me was the last place I wanted to be. I kept tugging on the risers, but before I could gather enough of my wits or wind to steer away, I shattered the dark surface of the earth and fell into a hole of darkness.

Shards of the earth rained around me. What odd hell was this?

I struggled to make sense of what was happening as I landed with a thud and hit the ground.

I was on a floor of some sort. There were walls.

I hadn't crashed through the earth at all. I'd fallen into a building.

In the dim light, I saw the outlines of large panes of glass above my head. They'd been broken not by me, but by the pack of explosives dangling below my legs. That was a miracle; the glass could easily have cut me to shreds. I had managed through luck to fall onto the roof of a greenhouse or some similar extension on the side of a stone building not far from the church, very close to the center of town.

And also very close to the gunfire and chaos outside.

I reached into my boot and cut off the leg pack as well as a small musette pack where I'd stuffed some toilet articles and rope. Yanking my gun from my chest, I found a door and ran out into a small yard; from there I went over a stone wall and found myself in the street.

How and why I was moving, I can't explain exactly. It's not just because those events are so distant in time. They were a blur then, too. I was moving partly on instinct, and partly on training. I knew my mission—get to Chef-du-Pont bridge. That was my entire goal, my whole purpose; if there was any logic involved in what I did at any given moment, it was wholly subconscious.

Somehow I knew that the bridge was some three miles away to the southwest. Somehow I knew to head in that direction. I sprinted across the yard, running as fast as I could. Gunfire came from every direction, including the churchyard and the cemetery, where a light machine gun was firing.

Shadows were everywhere. I caught a glimpse of one at the side of the steeple.

A shadow on the side.

No, a man.

Hanging halfway down?

Caught on something above.

Dead, surely.

The image registered in my brain, but at that moment there was nothing to be done, and it was just one more horror—one more obstacle to me getting down to the bridge and doing my job.

JOHN STEELE

If you are a World War II buff, you may already know that the paratrooper hanging from that steeple was John Steele. And in fact he wasn't dead—not when I saw him, and not later, either. He lived to tell his story.

In recent years, another part of the story has come to light, amid some controversy about exactly who did what at the church. I'm not the one to straighten it all out; whoever I saw, I thought was dead, and I didn't stick around to ask questions—or more likely, get shot myself.

But here's the story as I've come to understand it:

A fire started in the village near the center of town around 1 A.M., thanks to a stray bomb or incendiary. The entire town was alerted; citizens ran out and began putting out the fire. The German occupying force responded to supervise.

Aircraft carrying elements of the 82nd flew overhead a little more than an hour later, off course because of the fog and antiaircraft fire. By then, the fire was going great blazes, and the planes, low and silhouetted by the fire, were easy targets.

Antiaircraft guns in and around Sainte-Mère-Église began firing furiously. So did some of the Germans in the village itself.

Fifty paratroopers—maybe more—fell into the village. Many were shot at and pursued by the German force. Others got hung up in trees and were killed before they could get to the ground. A few drowned. One fell into the building that was on fire. He seems to have been carrying mortar rounds, which exploded, killing him if he hadn't already been shot or killed in the fall.

At least one man fell right on the church—John Steele, a private in the 2nd Battalion of the 505th. His chute snagged on the steeple, and there he hung, off the side, helpless to cut himself down. With Germans running back and forth, and citizens scrambling in every direction, Steele had the presence of mind to pretend to be dead—not easy, I'm sure, under the circumstances.

He hung there for quite a while—two hours at least—before the Germans discovered that he was still alive. At that point, they took him prisoner.

———————

For years, that was all most people knew of the story. But then other witnesses to the battle added more information concerning two other paratroopers who fell into Sainte-Mère-Église at roughly the same time, Private Ken Russell and Sergeant John Ray. Like Steele, they were members of F Company, and presumably would have jumped within moments of each other.

Russell also came down against the church building, crashing so hard that he nearly blacked out. His chute or the line was caught in the decorative gargoyles below the church roof; the snag left him dangling about twenty feet from the ground. He saw another man dangling above him nearby, though the man appeared to be dead.

The other man was, presumably, Steele, though in the darkness and under the circumstances, neither he nor anyone could be sure.

At roughly the same moment, Sergeant John Ray landed nearby. Ray was almost immediately shot by a German soldier and fell. The German then turned his attention to the church, where Russell and Steele were hanging. As he aimed his gun, he suddenly fell—Ray had managed to pull out his pistol and shoot the German.

Grateful to be alive, Russell cut his lines. Hobbled by the fall, he found Sergeant Ray dead. Thinking his two fellow soldiers were both gone, he went off looking for others in the stick or some place to hide.

Taken from the village before the 82nd liberated it, Steele managed to escape from the Germans a few days later. Though he told his story several times—and it became famous when Cornelius Ryan included it in his book about D-Day, *The Longest Day*—he apparently never mentioned either of the other two men. Russell seems not to have publicly shared his part for many years, either.

CHAOS OF BATTLE

I can understand why there are different versions of what happened that night. It would be shocking if there weren't.

My first few minutes in Sainte-Mère-Église were total chaos, a mental struggle to gain control or at least some bearings. People talk about the fog of war. I was in it, and the fog was very, very thick.

If there was a gun battle taking place around me, I don't remember it; I can't visualize it when I close my eyes. I can remember running, and the sounds of guns, and the weight of everything. The sweat in my clothes, the sense that I didn't want to die before I completed my mission.

My desire to do my job.

I believe I ran through the street without being shot at. This may not be true, since there were plenty of Germans around, though they seem to have been concentrated around the center of town. Whatever the case, I got out of the village without being hit; that much I know for sure.

Looking back once again in my mind's eye, what I see as I head out of town are several other paratroopers stuck in trees, already dead, shot before they could get out of their chutes. How many I saw, where exactly they were—at the outskirts of the village, in the field below it, along the road to Chef-du-Pont—I can't say. The only thing that remains intact is the terror. I still feel the emptiness that comes with recognizing a fellow soldier, a buddy, is dead.

I found a road and headed in the direction of the bridge. According to the map, the Chef-du-Pont bridge would have been about three miles from where I landed, beyond the little hamlet that gave the bridge its name. How long it took to find that road and how far along the road I got—and even if it was the right road to the bridge—I didn't know then, and I can't tell now. But to the best I can remember, I hadn't gotten all that far out of the village when I came upon a group of other paratroopers who'd landed and were organizing themselves.

I found they were heading to the bridge, so I joined them. There were between thirty and fifty of us all told; it was hard to tell in the dark.

A lot has been written about the tin crickets we used to communicate that night, and the code words and such. The crickets were pieces of tin like a kid's toy, which made a clicking sound when you clicked it. We were supposed to click once from cover, then wait for the recognition signal—two clicks. Or, if you lost your clicker, you could give the code word "flash"; "thunder" was the right response.

I didn't do any of that. Meeting this group was the only time it would have been necessary, and it was obvious who we were, and a few words would have made it clear any way.

We started moving toward Chef-du-Pont. The core of the group, or at least the leaders, were from Company F, but the rest was a real mishmash. I think there were soldiers from the 508th as well as the 505th, and it's even possible a man or two had jumped with the 101st Airborne Division, which would have put him very far off course. In the scramble of the drop, people landed in all sorts of places. You worked with whoever you could find, doing whatever needed to be done. We all knew that the bridges were among the main objectives.

At some point the group I was with split in half and began walking on the roadside and in the fields flanking the road. We were spread out to avoid being surprised, and to make it easier to attack any Germans using the road. The fields were lower than the road, with mounds or underbrush dividing them from the pavement. The height varied, but the entire stretch was perfect for an ambush.

We hadn't gone too far when we heard the sound of two or three vehicles heading in our direction.

It took moments to get into a position for an ambush.

The little convoy included a couple of trucks and a *kettenkrad*, a light towing vehicle. The trucks were moving slowly, easy targets—and within moments, the drivers and the few passengers were dead.

It was the first time I'd shot at someone for real. I don't know that I killed anyone; I don't even know for certain that I hit any of the Germans, though I certainly believe I did.

That night was still speeding by, events all in a rush, too quick to analyze. I was still green, unused to it all, running on adrena-line.

We took the *kettenkrad* to use, and piled some of the shells and explosives that had been in a truck into the back. They would be very useful for blowing the bridge.

What's a *kettenkrad*?

You might describe the German vehicle as the bastard child of a motorcycle and tank. The front end had a single wheel like a motorcycle; the back was an open chassis on tank treads. Just big enough for two men to sit in the back while another steered at the front, it did the job that today's soldiers use ATVs for.

One of the paratroopers got in the front and began steering, tentatively, down the road. Four or five of us walked along with him, spreading out once more—with the *kettenkrad*, we were the ones who could be easily ambushed.

———————

I don't know why the Germans hadn't been more alert, why they didn't suspect there might be an ambush. Why they thought they were safe.

We had no illusions.

———————

The *kettenkrad* moved slowly. I was on the right side of the road alone a few minutes later when we heard machine gun fire. It took another few seconds to realize bullets were flying in our direc-tion. Everyone ducked for cover.

The gunfire was coming from about a hundred yards away. That may sound like a lot, but it was well within the range of a German machine gun. Fortunately in the dark and the tangled vegetation, we weren't easy targets. I quickly realized that I was on the opposite side of the road from whoever was firing at us, and began advancing, trying to catch a glimpse of what we were up against.

I soon saw that we were not fighting a machine gun nest at all. It was a German tank.

I wasn't thinking straight enough to be scared. I didn't feel anything, really, not fear and certainly not joy. I just started acting automatically, as I'd practiced in training. I moved in the direction of the tank, flanking it, somehow confident that I wasn't going to get shot at.

A plan formed in my head: I'd run past the tank to the end of the road where it formed a T intersection. I'd cross and come up behind it. There I could shoot the man who was working the machine gun in the turret, and then either find some way to immobilize the tank or wait for my companions to help.

The clatter of the machine gun would keep the Germans from hearing me. They probably wouldn't see me, either. They'd be too busy trying to kill the men they'd pinned down. It was dark, and I was coming from an unexpected direction.

Everything went perfectly—until I reached the end of the road, rounded the corner, and promptly fell into a slit trench.

There was a German soldier not two feet from me, looking down the road where my companions were trapped. He turned.

That face I remember. Other details of that night, like so many details, I have forgotten or even distorted, but that face, I will not forget. A young man, probably my age. Surprised, and yes, scared.

I shot him. Two bullets.

I didn't and don't know if I'd killed anyone earlier, but this man I know I killed.

I'm not bragging. It was my job. It was war. I would soon kill many other men, some so close I could feel their breath. So many men that most would fade quickly, or not even make an impression. But this man I won't forget.

The soldier was a grenadier, and in his slit trench he had a Panzerfaust—the bazooka-like weapon that I'd learned to fire in England.

I left him but took his weapon and moved across the road so that I was behind the tank, which was sitting on the side of the road a short distance from the T. I couldn't tell in the dark exactly what kind of tank it was; the Germans had both Tigers and Panzer IVs in Normandy, along with heavy Panthers and lighter repurposed French Renaults.

If I had to guess, I'd say Tiger. Whatever it was, it was big and dark, and shooting at my buddies.

I crept closer. I was probably a bit too close, as I think about it now, but . . .

The shell hit square in the back of the tank. It didn't destroy it, or kill the crew—a few moments later, the hatchway popped open and they began climbing out.

By then I'd thrown down the Panzerfaust and grabbed my Thompson. The explosion had dazed them; they were close and disoriented, unsure what was going on.

Within a few seconds they lay on the ground, bleeding profusely or already dead; I didn't stop to check, running instead to get the rest of my guys.

TO TOWN AND BACK

With the intersection cleared, I joined the others heading to Chef-du-Pont. We reached a group that had dug in above the bridge-head, which was now in American control. I was told that we had the bridge, and there'd be no need for me to blow it up. Instead I was ordered to dig a foxhole. Not long after I finished, the group I'd hooked up with was ordered to join other paratroopers who were rallying to take Sainte-Mère-Église.

It turned out that the bridge at Chef-du-Pont was not taken that night; in fact, it would take two more days and a lot of blood before it was secured. But that is the fog of war—information is at a premium, and good information is sometimes nonexistent.

The battle at Sainte-Mère-Église had actually started a good hour or more before we landed, when the building I'd seen on fire had first begun to burn. The Frenchmen trying to put it out were stunned to see aircraft flying overhead, followed by the round circles of parachutes and the constant *ack-ack* of the nearby anti-aircraft guns. The Germans who controlled the town shooed the townspeople back to their houses and began gunning down the paratroopers.

I had jumped in after the first serial or wave of paratroopers. By then the fire was going strong, and the Germans were probably concentrating on killing the injured paratroopers in the surrounding fields and the edge of town. Jumping low and fast was hazardous, but jumping from aircraft that were too high could be just as bad. If you lost a few panels on your chute—which could happen for different reasons—you fell even harder. The darkness made it close to impossible to prepare for your landing. A hard landing could mean a broken leg or hip. If you were stuck in a tree, odds were good that you'd be shot before you got out of the harness.

But enough of our guys managed to group together outside of town to run out the small contingent of German defenders as the night wore on, and by the time I arrived, Lieutenant Colonel Ed Krause had hung his American flag up at town hall. The colonel had hoisted it around 0430, hours ahead of schedule—he'd promised to get the flag up by nightfall. The colonel had flown the same flag in Sicily and Naples; he was another one of our lead-from-the-front guys.

Seeing that flag made me feel pretty proud.

There were other sights, though, that didn't. Paratroopers hung by their lines from trees, and bodies—American, German, and French civilians—were scattered around. At no point that first night, or any of those nights, did I ever feel safe. The history books may make it seem as if we were in a very secure position, with a guaranteed win. I felt the exact opposite. I was constantly worried about having enough ammunition. I saw how tired and pressed other guys were, and wondered if I looked the same. If the Germans managed to mount a large attack against the town or one of the bridges, we would be in big trouble.

I knew I'd do what had to be done. I just worried it wouldn't be enough.

———————————

There is no good way to die in war. But of all the horrible ways men fell that night, one of the worst had to be by drowning.

As part of their defense system, the Germans had flooded fields throughout the region. The water was several feet deep in places; beneath it, the ground was a mucky quicksand. A number of paratroopers died when they descended into the flooded fields around the peninsula and drowned.

We knew that the Germans had flooded areas near the beaches, narrowing the usable terrain so much that the roads were like thin causeways, greatly restricting movement. We didn't realize how much they had flooded inland, too.

Why not? One theory is that it was difficult to detect in the aerial photos at the time.

Thinking back, flooding the fields probably hurt the Germans a lot more than us. If they hadn't turned some of the farm fields into swamps and shallow lakes, they might have been able to send tanks to ford the river and really given us headaches. Maybe we would have come up with another way to defeat them; there are many variables in war.

There were other hazards besides the flooded lands. The Germans had planted fields with what became known as Rommel's Asparagus—wooden stakes or posts a few feet high with mines posted on top. Placed to discourage glider assaults, landing on one was a death sentence.

Though I'd been trained to disarm mines, I didn't have to deal with any that night. That may just have been the luck of the draw, because there were plenty around. The Germans had a number of nasty devices, none more so than the "Bouncin' Betty." This was an antipersonnel mine typically buried in a field. It looked like a coffee can with a metal tube sticking out the top. The tube was part of the trigger mechanism, attached to a tripwire or pressure sensor. Once triggered, the mine shot upward, then exploded about groin-high. Steel balls or scrap metal would shoot out, often catching its unlucky victims in the privates or nearby torso and legs. The mines were quite lethal; we'd been taught in training that the spray could wound or even kill at 450 feet.

These mines had a simple safing mechanism; you stuck a small pin into a hole near the trigger at the top and it could not go off. Finding them, though, could be hard. Without a metal detector, you would have to get down close to the ground and probe with a knife. While it was safer to be on the ground when one of the mines went off—in hopes that the exploding cloud of shrapnel would miss you—probing a field for the devices was as nerve-racking as it was time consuming.

The Germans also had these wooden mines, the Schu-mine 42. They were geniuses with these. You couldn't find it with a metal detector. You had to use your eyes, look for signs in the terrain. Or maybe you'd know there were mines because of warning signs. Then you could poke around very, very carefully.

You'd find one mine and start probing with a bayonet to find where it was at, feel around to get the dimensions, make sure there were no wires or anything to trip or connect it to another mine. But you had to be extra careful, because sometimes these mines were booby-trapped, one on top of the other. Move the top and the bottom explodes.

There were other hazards that night, though far less fatal, related to some humorous stories, though I'm sure they weren't very funny at the time. Several paratroopers were spooked by "enemy" cows in the field. A few landed in odd but not life-threatening positions—though there I guess my greenhouse probably takes the prize. Blame the odd landings on darkness, or the wind, or just accept that strange things happen in war, especially to paratroopers.

––––––––––––––

By daybreak on June 6, the men down at the beaches were dealing with much worse obstacles, especially on Omaha. Shortly after 0600, the first landing craft had touched the rocky bottoms in front of Sainte-Honorine, Saint-Laurent, Vierville, Colleville—towns whose names would soon be inscribed in bold in the histories of the 1st and 29th Division. They'd been met with murderous gunfire, mortar shells, and artillery.

It took hours and many deaths for the soldiers to reach the few cuts that led to the high ground above. Hand-to-hand fighting and sheer willpower finally gave the troops there enough of a foothold to consider the invasion a success by late in the afternoon.

Things were easier on Utah, the beach closest to us. Some credit for their success may have come from a mistake: the landing craft carrying part of the 8th Infantry's 2nd Battalion were driven far south of their targeted landing zone. They landed anyway, found opposition relatively light, and immediately plunged inland. Other landing craft followed to this location; by 0830 the landing area was secure and American forces were headed inland. Our brother troopers in the 101st Airborne had taken Poupeville, securing a key causeway and route way from the water. The Germans set up stiff defenses at Sainte-Marie-du-Mont, threatening another key exit from the beach; it would take several hours of house-to-house fighting to secure the area.

Farther east, the British and Canadians landed successfully, but German defenses kept them from reaching Caen, a key if optimistic Day 1 objective. Caen would turn out to be a far more difficult target than British commanding general Bernard Montgomery and his planners had believed; resistance there would eventually change Allied plans completely.

———————

As day broke in Sainte-Mère-Église, we could hear low thuds of thunder from the beachhead. The noise sounded more like the thump of a bass drum than anything dangerous. In reality, they were the shocks of large naval shells being called down on German strongholds like pillboxes and artillery emplacements.

We couldn't afford to pay much attention to those salvos, though; we were soon under attack on both the north and south ends of town.

North of town, the 505th's 2nd Battalion machine guns repelled a German counterattack using grenades as well as machine guns. A group of mortarmen arriving with full ammo bags—rare that day—helped stave off the Germans. Members of the 307th Combat Engineers came up to that fight; we lost one of our lieutenants, Alexander Sweeney, in the gun battle.

I was down on the west side of the village, trying to get ammo from the dead and wounded and recover some of the ammo packages that had been dropped the night before. The Germans had started shelling the town, and then around 10 A.M. they attacked with self-propelled guns on a main road, N-13, near Fauville, south of Sainte-Mère-Église.

The battle was a mishmash of confused action, but in the end, the Germans withdrew. That was the last time they tried taking that road—though the attacks on Sainte-Mère-Église were far from over.

Around midafternoon, a German truck tried rolling through a position on the main road southwest of town. It hit a mine set by some of our boys earlier. That stopped the truck—and the men trying to come in behind it. Not long after that, a group of Germans tried trickery rather than force to get in—waving a recognition panel they had found, they pretended to be paratroopers with some German prisoners. Fortunately, the real paratroopers on the southwest side realized what was going on and opened fire.

The worst attacks were to the north, where a platoon led by Lieutenant Turner Turnbell came under heavy attack at Neuville-au-Plain. Around five that evening, they were nearly caught by a German attack on their flank. Fortunately, the Germans were surprised by another platoon that had snuck into position and beat back the Germans with the help of mortar barrages.

The Germans never got a chance to renew their attack that night, thanks to some heavy rounds from a battleship offshore. But at first light the next day, grenadiers renewed the attack with self-propelled guns and artillery.

Meanwhile, we got it on the southwest. As historian Phil Nordyke puts it, we were caught in a vise.

German tanks at the south began advancing across the open road. But here we were helped by the Germans' defensive tactics. The flooded fields as well as the hedgerows narrowed the passages they could use. By now we had some 57 mm howitzers in town; they stopped the German tanks and trucks with some well-placed hits; what they didn't get, our bazooka men took care of. Once the road was choked, the German advance faltered.

The guys at the north weren't nearly so lucky. Lieutenant Turnbull was killed; his men and the others there, low on ammunition, were hard-pressed. Then, somewhere in the afternoon, five

American tanks galloped through Sainte-Mère-Église, guided by Pathfinders who were riding rodeo-style on top. The troopers had reached the 4th Division and convinced their commander to send reinforcements.

By 5 P.M., the tanks were in position with some fresh paratroopers to mount a counterattack on the Germans. By nightfall, the German unit that had pressed the attack had been laid to waste, with most of its equipment destroyed, and a good number of dead, wounded, and POWs.

I don't remember sleeping those first two or three days; I ran on pure adrenaline. I might have been too scared to relax, even for a brief nap. This was my first time in combat, and I was trying to make sense of it all, do what I was told, and stay alive. Not in that order.

A few guys had taken pills to help them stay awake, but that sort of thing wasn't for me. Other guys were so tired I saw them just drop to the ground and fall into a slumber.

It's hard to get used to taking ammo from the dead. You do it. But you're never at ease. Bullets were the most important, of course, but we also got food, K Rations, and D Bars. A lot of guys took cigarettes, not just to smoke but to trade or just give to the civilians.

If we didn't feel like we had enough ammunition, we absolutely didn't feel like we had enough firepower. One 75—a light howitzer or cannon—came in on a glider, and there were some heavier machine guns. A few German weapons were also "liberated" for our use.

General Ridgway set up division quarters in the village, commanding the defense. He didn't have a usable radio; messages were passed by runners. General Gavin, who was overseeing the fights at du-Pont and further north at La Fière, had the same problem.

The officers consolidated the units as best they could. I was now unofficially infantry, attached to an ad hoc squad of "regular" paratroopers. I was available to blow up a target or defuse a mine, but in the meantime I was a gunner, doing what needed to be done. We kept picking up men who had parachuted far from the intended drop zones over the next few days, as well as guys who had been holed up hiding from nearby Germans.

Still, in my opinion we were short on manpower and didn't have the communications we would have loved to have to communicate between groups.

Nowadays, the Army has wonderful communications; back then it was more hope and prayer.

THE BRIDGES

While Sainte-Mère-Église was at the center of the fighting those first few days, the two bridges nearby at Chef-du-Pont and La Fière remained contested.

Though du-Pont looked secure when I got there the night of June 6, it was anything but. True, we had guys on the east side that could ambush anything coming across, but the Germans held the west.

And a bit of the north, as some of our troopers found when they approached a little after I was ordered back to Sainte-Mère-Église.

General Gavin led an attack on a train filled with German troops near a station north of du-Pont soon after landing; after that, some of the men coming down from the north found Germans dug in around a farm about a thousand yards north of the bridge. A grenade and rifle duel followed; the Germans brought up artillery and men and got to within six hundred yards of our men before they were stopped.

The next day, a glider came in with a 57 mm gun; the gun and a platoon of men shook off the Germans and secured the east side approach. But the Germans remained on the west side of the causeway, contesting the bridge that afternoon before finally being driven off.

Credit for finally taking the bridge is usually shared in the history books by the 325th Glider Infantry Regiment, the third battalion of the 508th Parachute Regiment, and the 90th Infantry Division's 1st Battalion of the 358th Infantry Regiment; a lot of men bled for that piece of real estate.

––––––––––––

Down at La Fière Bridge, an even more intense back-and-forth battle took shape. By the end of June 6, the 505th had men on both banks—but not on the bridge itself. The Germans were particularly strong on the west side.

Company B of the 307th Engineers—my "parent" unit—came in on June 7, reinforcing the battalion on the north side of the bridge. An ad hoc group of paratroopers who had grouped together were cut down when they tried to join those forces by moving across a swamp from the west side.

By daybreak, everyone in the area knew there would be a counterattack. It came around ten in the morning, when the Germans tried to force the bridge with a couple of Renault tanks and two hundred men. The Americans were being blanketed by artillery and mortar fire, but managed to get out in the open long enough to stop the tanks on the causeway with bazookas and a 57 mm gun that had been rolled in off a glider.

Our losses were severe, but apparently the Germans were even worse—they asked for a cease-fire to collect their dead.

Tanks from the 4th Division and men from the 325 Glider Infantry Regiment arrived, setting the stage for a fierce battle on June 8. Engineers taped out a route through the marshes for the attack. Once again, the attack failed to clear the entire bridge.

Somewhere around there, we were marched up to help. My unit was placed in reserve, waiting for a German counterattack. Ammo must have been getting very tight, because the officer we were with told us not to shoot unless we were certain we had a target in sight.

General Gavin decided we were taking that bridge by brute force. He put the 3rd Battalion of 325th in front, and around ten thirty the morning of June 9, they charged, running behind an artillery barrage some 750 yards across open fields with mortars, machine guns, and God only knows what firing at them.

I didn't see this bit firsthand, but it was during that battle for La Fière that Charles N. DeGlopper earned his Medal of Honor. Private DeGlopper was the first soldier from the 82nd awarded the medal during World War II. DeGlopper sacrificed himself providing covering fire for the rest of his unit, enabling the bridge to be taken.

This is his citation, with a description of what happened:

He was a member of Company C, 325th Glider Infantry, on 9 June 1944 advancing with the forward platoon to secure a bridgehead across the Merderet River at La Fière, France. At dawn the platoon had penetrated an outer line of machineguns and riflemen, but in so doing had become cut off from the rest of the company. Vastly superior forces began a decimation of the stricken unit and put in motion a flanking maneuver which would have completely exposed the American platoon in a shallow roadside ditch where it had taken cover. Detecting this danger, Pfc. DeGlopper volunteered to support his comrades by fire from his automatic rifle while they attempted a withdrawal through a break in a hedgerow 40 yards to the rear. Scorning a concentration of enemy automatic weapons and rifle fire, he walked from the ditch onto the road in full view of the Germans, and sprayed the hostile positions with assault fire. He was wounded, but he continued firing. Struck again, he started to fall; and yet his grim determination and valiant fighting spirit could not be broken. Kneeling in the roadway, weakened by his grievous wounds, he leveled his heavy weapon against the enemy and fired burst after burst until killed outright. He was successful in drawing the enemy action away from his fellow soldiers, who continued the fight from a more advantageous position and established the first bridgehead over the Merderet. In the area where he made his intrepid stand his comrades later found the ground strewn with dead Germans and many machineguns and automatic weapons which he had knocked out of action. Pfc. DeGlopper's gallant sacrifice and unflinching heroism while facing insurmountable odds were in great measure responsible for a highly important tactical victory in the Normandy Campaign.

The paratroopers who followed DeGlopper had to pick their way past bodies, destroyed vehicles, and mines. After they gained a foothold, engineers came in to remove some of the obstacles. Unfortunately in the confusion, a tank rushing to join the battle on the other side hit a mine that hadn't been cleared. Not only was it destroyed, but the explosion killed or hurt a bunch of men nearby.

Still, by noon, the causeway and both sides were ours. The Germans kept up their artillery and mortar fire, but we weren't about to be dislodged, now that our objectives had finally been taken.

———————————

D-Day had been costly. For the 82nd, the total was 156 killed, 347 wounded, and 756 missing. If you figure that 6,240 men made the jump, the numbers work out to a casualty rate of 20 percent. The total represents about a tenth of all casualties suffered by the Allies during D-Day. The 101st Division suffered similar losses: 182 killed, 557 wounded, and 501 missing, according to Army historical records.

Soldiers weren't the only ones who were killed. The people of France paid a terrible price for their liberation. In Sainte-Mère-Église alone, forty-three civilians died from May to August; eighteen were killed on D-Day alone. Errant bombs and stray bullets were certainly a hazard, but the village was also deliberately targeted because our troops were there. Artillery shells did not discriminate between fighter and civilian. Often when we think of war we forget how much those who aren't fighting suffer, and what they must do to survive. They risk their lives just by being alive.

And yet the French that I met over the next few days went out of their way to help us. I can't count the number of people who offered food. One Frenchwoman, spotting a soldier using a rifle as a cane, retrieved a crutch from her house and gave it to him.

There are any number of stories of GIs being kissed—didn't happen to me, sorry to say. More seriously, civilians led us to arms depots and gave us intelligence that would have been impossible to gather from anywhere else.

One Frenchwoman came out of her house with sausages she'd hidden from the Germans. And someone else introduced us to Calvados—an alcoholic French drink made from apples; it's a kind of apple brandy made in the region and it packs a good punch.

Milk was my drink of choice. Whenever anyone offered, I would drink my fill. Coming from the Midwest and farm country, I guess that's not surprising.

The Germans of the 709th Division are sometimes criticized by historians for being poor fighters. Personally, I can't say that. Most of them fought pretty hard. They'd been in the area long enough to train and prepare defenses, and I'd say they learned well.

One thing about their defenses. If you pushed them back, you could count on them counterattacking the next day, or sometimes sooner. They were scrappy fighters.

The German paratroopers we faced were even tougher. The youngest soldiers had grown up in Hitler's time and were dedicated to the Nazi regime and Hitler. They were very, very dedicated to the fatherland. Oh yeah, I have to say, they were good soldiers.

There was one weakness common to all the soldiers—if their leaders were dead or missing, they were in trouble. I think we were better at improvising, whether in small groups or alone. That was our training.

"HELL OF A WAR"

———————

Those first few days in Normandy were confused, hectic, and very dangerous. Allied troops were pouring into France, but we still had only a bare toehold. The Germans had finally figured out that this was the main invasion, and they threw what they had against us. Rommel was back on the scene. As we were quickly learning, the hedgerow country was filled with natural defenses. The ancient farm fields were divided by high mounds of dirt and foliage, built up over centuries. They gave defenders plenty of cover.

Geography worked both ways, though. Paratroopers had died in the flooded fields, but that same water meant the Germans had to stick to the roads when they moved against us, making them easy targets for ambush or for our aircraft flying above. The hedgerows were another barrier farther inland; where fences or even low stone walls could be easily knocked down, these thick mounds were like moats, once more restricting heavy travel to the roads.

———————

Over the years, the blur of those first forty-eight or seventy-some hours has only become worse. But there are a few things I remember quite well, even though I can't quite place them in the timeline.

I believe this happened around the time I was at du Pont or La Fière, when I'd been told to dig a foxhole as a defensive position. I did just that, and clambered in, glad for a few moments of rest with no one firing at me.

That didn't last.

We started taking artillery. As I hunkered down in my foxhole, another soldier jumped in.

"Hey, son, this is a hell of a war," said the man.

The bombardment stopped after a few seconds. The man got up and went off.

God as my witness, the man was General Gavin.

A hell of a war. Yes.

FIVE

Hedgerows

HELL ON EARTH

Back home, the newspapers and radio stations blasted the news:

Allied troops were back in France.

The early reports were not very accurate—the news was being censored to avoid giving the enemy too much information, and most eyewitness reports from the journalists on the scene would not come for several days. But they did give people the most important facts: we had opened up another front in the war, and gained a toehold in Europe.

That evening, President Roosevelt addressed the nation via radio, asking all Americans to pray with him.

Almighty God: Our sons, pride of our Nation, this day have set upon a mighty endeavor, a struggle to preserve our Republic, our religion, and our civilization, and to set free a suffering humanity.

Lead them straight and true; give strength to their arms, stoutness to their hearts, steadfastness in their faith.

*They will need Thy blessings. Their road will be long and hard.
For the enemy is strong. He may hurl back our forces. Success may
not come with rushing speed, but we shall return again and again;
and we know that by Thy grace, and by the righteousness of our
cause, our sons will triumph.*

*They will be sore tried, by night and by day, without rest—until
the victory is won. The darkness will be rent by noise and flame.
Men's souls will be shaken with the violences of war.*

*For these men are lately drawn from the ways of peace. They
fight not for the lust of conquest. They fight to end conquest. They
fight to liberate. They fight to let justice arise, and tolerance and
good will among all Thy people. They yearn but for the end of battle, for their return to the haven of home.*

*Some will never return. Embrace these, Father, and receive them,
Thy heroic servants, into Thy kingdom.*

*And for us at home—fathers, mothers, children, wives, sisters,
and brothers of brave men overseas—whose thoughts and prayers
are ever with them—help us, Almighty God, to rededicate ourselves
in renewed faith in Thee in this hour of great sacrifice.*

Arlene had no way of knowing that I was in the middle of it.
She suspected it, especially when the reports began saying that
paratroopers were involved.

"I just figure he's coming back," she kept telling her family and
friends.

She prayed. She worked. She helped her mother and father take
care of the younger kids. She prayed at night for me. What else
could she do?

My assignment after D-Day was to stay with the "regular" paratroopers, using my skills as an engineer where needed, disabling mines and booby traps, or setting explosives. I don't remember defusing any mines, but I did disable a number of booby traps we found in houses—mostly easy ones, so hastily set that you could see the tripwire. Of course, if you missed . . .

A Luger on the ground, attached to a small explosive—pick it up and boom. A cord running across the hallway; kick it and *karroom*. Usually these things were so obvious that only an extremely careless soldier not paying attention would have tripped them—and inside a building, everyone paid attention.

For all intents and purposes, I was just an infantryman filling out a platoon, armed with my submachinegun and doing what I was told. Things were very ad hoc the first few days, and even in the weeks that followed. I think we all accepted that as normal. It fit in with what I had experienced in training, where I'd been assigned to work with different groups. Whether things were organized exactly as command wanted, I couldn't tell you. I just followed orders.

With troops from the 4th Division reaching Sainte-Mère-Église and the surrounding area, I was assigned to help get supplies from Utah Beach. I went down with a few other guys in a borrowed 4th Division Jeep to pick up ammunition and whatever else we could grab.

I don't know what Utah looked like when the infantry first landed. When I got there a few days later, it had been transformed into a massive staging area. Pictures don't tell half the story. It was littered with destroyed vehicles and armaments. There was enough junk on the beach to fight another war. Wrecked vehicles. Wrecked artillery.

Wrecked men.

Horrors of war. Things I saw in those early days are too horrible to describe, or even remember clearly. Men's heads split open in gliders that had crashed. Drowned bodies half-floating in shallow water.

Hell on earth.

At the same time, the area hummed with troops. At the beach, trucks and DUKW amphibious vehicles shuttled things from landing craft and small boats. Tanks and artillery were hustled to the forward area. We had a foothold in France, and we weren't leaving.

ADVANCING

If anyone thought that the 82nd had earned a rotation back to England to rest, they were sadly mistaken. After regrouping, we were given a new objective, a town a few miles away.

I'm sorry, but I can't remember now that name of the village. We moved through so many in the days and weeks that followed, each one a little different, each one almost the same. You would think that the names would have burned themselves into my brain somehow, but time has erased them.

We were supposed to be working with a regiment in the 4th Division. We waited for them to show up at a rendezvous point; when they didn't, our commander decided we would move out anyway. Whether he thought the 4th Division guys would show up later or not, I couldn't say.

The road we took initially led straight to the village, but well before we reached it, the officer found a narrower side road that looked as if it wasn't defended. We took that; a short time later the scouts told us that they'd spotted a large group of Germans gathering in a field ahead, just outside the village we were going to attack. It wasn't clear what the Germans were up to—resting, maybe, or organizing a counterattack—but there were hundreds of them.

The way terrain worked, they were gathered below a thick stand of brush, almost as if they were in a bowl. Our commanders had us spread out along what would be the lip of the bowl; at a given signal, everyone opened fire.

It was a slaughter.

Some of the Germans tried surrendering. A lot of guys kept firing. Our NCOs and officers had a hard time getting our men to stop shooting. After a few days of fighting and seeing our friends get killed in ugly ways, we weren't long on mercy. But eventually the gunfire did stop, and we took prisoners.

By the time we got to the town, it had been almost totally abandoned; maybe the Germans had left two or three men. We had no trouble securing the place.

Most of our operations in the "bocage," or hedgerow, country were not nearly that easy. While I've forgotten the names of the small villages where we fought, I haven't forgotten how murderous the hedgerows could be, or how a tiny hamlet of no more than three or four houses could become a death trap.

I would guess that if you hear the word "hedge," you think of a nice little piece of greenery in front of a house. It might be two feet high. Even if it were taller, you wouldn't think of it as much of a barrier to fighting men.

The hedgerows in France were nothing like that. They were more like tall berms that could tower over a man's head, topped with thick rows of trees, bushes, and other vegetation. Built up over years, they were strengthened by the thick roots of the trees and brush, like reinforcement rods in concrete. Getting across the hedgerows was not impossible, but it took time and it was difficult for a mass of men to do all at once. And as soon as you were in the clear, you were an easy target.

These berms were natural points of defense. When they flanked a road, they provided a good place for an ambush. When they surrounded a field, which they usually did, they turned the field into a killing box. There were usually only one or two openings into the field; these were easily guarded or watched. The German defenders had their mortars and artillery zeroed in on the field, so that anyone starting across could be hit. They arranged their machine guns so that attackers would be caught in a crossfire.

They were good, those German soldiers.

The farm buildings near or in these fields were mostly stone. The Germans were famous for putting machine guns in them. Our bullets would bounce off harmlessly. The approaches would be well covered; often without heavy weapons it could take quite a lot of time to get near enough to the house to toss in a grenade or enter through an unguarded door or window.

The minute we'd break out of the hedgerows, we'd be ducking machine gun fire. All we could do was hope our legs were pumping good enough, and that we could get across the field without getting hit, or hit too badly. Run straight, run fast.

The intelligence people and high command missed how tough

these were going to be. Tanks weren't much help—they would climb over, exposing their lightly armored undersides as easy targets.

Things got a little better when a smart-thinking sergeant came up with the idea of welding metal prongs on the front of tanks. They looked like big forks or rhino tusks sticking out of the front—which led guys to call the tanks "Rhinos." The tusks allowed the armor to go through the hedgerows rather than over them. The tanks could plow through the hedgerows like bulldozers, opening doors where the Germans least expected.

I never worked with the rhinos myself. I did see one or two, and I could imagine they'd do a heck of a job—but I would have hated to be in the tank when they rammed the hedgerow. I think you'd get shuffled around more than a little bit. Some of those looked thicker than a castle wall. Rattle your brain.

It wasn't good tank country, but the men manning the tanks seemed to deal with it just fine. They needed the infantry to keep them from being easily picked off by soldiers in ambush; we needed them to break through tough defenses.

"You don't have to worry about the little stuff," I told a crew member one day while we were catching a break. "You only have to worry about the big bullets. We're worrying about everything."

"Join us," he said.

I looked at the tank. It was nice, but would I want to spend a whole day in one? Let alone a week or a month?

"I have a better job," I told him.

They did have better food—C Rations, where we had K Rations. Pineapple in a can. Weenies—canned hot dogs.

Not good enough to get me to change my job, though.

This wasn't a noble fight.

There was one battle where the Germans put up a white flag and said they wanted a cease-fire to collect the wounded and the dead. Our officers agreed.

We had one aid man—a combat medic who tended to the wounded on the battlefield. He went out to help our guys.

Don't you know they shot our aid man after they had finished taking their people off the field?

I don't think we took many prisoners after that.

TO THE DOUVE

The Allies had gained a foothold in Normandy on D-Day, successfully landing on all of the beaches and setting the stage for a massive buildup. A crude landing strip was established in the Utah area by nightfall; many would follow. Fresh men and supplies were landed in a variety of naval boats—large landing craft drove up on the shore to offload tanks and men, then backed out with the wounded. The vaunted 21st Panzer Division attempted to drive the British back to the sea, only to be cut to shreds by the ground troops and a ferocious air attack.

In the seven days following the landings, a total of three hundred thousand men would come through the Allied beaches and makeshift airstrips. Tanks arrived in droves. Artillery, critical to the Army's tactics and strategy, began pounding German positions, helping infantry advance and paralyzing counterstrikes.

But the Germans had succeeded in blocking Caen from the

British. They had lost Sainte-Mère-Église, but still held Cherbourg at the tip of the Cotentin Peninsula. Though their divisions near the battlefield had been battered, they were rushing reinforcements forward, hitting us where they thought we were weak. The 12th SS Panzer Division and the Panzer Lehr Division—two of the best-equipped units Rommel had—sped to the front. Other units rushed forward by any means possible—truck, train, even bicycle. Rommel was back in France, organizing his defense and counterstrikes. And while they had been fooled about our intent, now they guessed at our plans—orders were given to destroy the port in Cherbourg in hopes that we could not use it to supply our armies. Some 40,000 German troops were north of us in the Cotentin Peninsula, defending Cherbourg and aiming to throw the troops coming in at Utah back out to sea.

American troops had suffered great losses; the estimates on D-Day alone amount to 8,200 casualties; many were men I'd trained with. And while we had many successes in those first few days, we actually fell short of what had originally been planned. The Germans were fighting tough, and the defenses of the hedgerows multiplied their ferociousness. Rather than fighting in swift strokes, much of the Allied army had to slug it out in small unit fights where taking over a few hundred yards could take hours if not an entire day.

Airborne units are often taken out of a battle to refit and regroup after ground units reach them, but that didn't happen to us. Instead, the 82nd and the 101st stayed to help cut off the Cotentin Peninsula.

We were tasked with extending and holding the line to the

Douve River, west of where the 101st was operating. While the Merderet, our objective the first night, flows north–south in the Cotentin Peninsula, the Douve meanders east to west, then north. Like the Merderet, the Germans had allowed the river to flood the lowlands, forming a natural barrier from the Utah beaches westward. The flooding had widened the river to almost lake-like widths in some spots. Though the water was relatively shallow, it couldn't be easily crossed in many areas without a boat or taking a bridge.

Seven miles southeast of Sainte-Mère-Église, the city of Carentan sat at the base of the Douve, connected to the nearby ocean by a canal. Though technically a channel port because of the canal, the facilities there were not sufficient for the size ships needed to deliver supplies. But it was still strategic.

A small city—the population was estimated to be about four thousand—Carentan was located between the Omaha and Utah beaches; main roads to both ran through it. A rail line connected it with Cherbourg. It could easily become the fulcrum in an attack against either beachhead, or a strongpoint meant to keep them separate.

The 101st was charged with seizing Carentan. Collecting as many of its scattered units and soldiers as it could, the division launched the attack June 10. Combat engineers with the 502 Regiment played an important role opening the bridges and forging the canals during the three-day battle; after the city was taken, the Germans launched a ferocious counterattack with tanks that nearly pushed through the city. The timely arrival of elements of the 2nd Armored Division (thrown into battle because of secret message intercepts) routed the Germans, crushing much of the 37th SS Panzergrenadier and 17th SS Panzer Battalion.

With the 101st in control, we moved westward, part of the thrust to cut off the top of the peninsula and prevent the Germans from reinforcing Carentan. Saint-Sauveur-le-Vicomte, about ten miles west of Sainte-Mère-Église as the crow flies, became a key American objective. After the 9th Infantry Division bogged down attacking the city, the 505th Regimental Combat Team was thrown into the battle.

By that point, about a week after D-Day, I'd rejoined the platoon I'd jumped with. There were a lot of new faces—no less than a quarter of the original group had been killed, and very possibly more were gone. There were a lot of people I'd never seen before, not even in line for chow.

On June 14, the 82nd began moving in the direction of Saint-Sauveur-le-Vicomte. A lot of small battles slowed us down. Taking a small hamlet like Les Rosiers—which even today has fewer than a dozen buildings—took an entire day.

The Germans set up tanks and artillery pieces as well as machine guns in and behind the buildings, and covered the fields from hedgerows, making it impossible to come down roads until they were run out. The destruction everywhere was horrific. You'd see tanks on fire when you passed a crossroad; often the body of a crewman or two would smolder nearby.

Saint-Sauveur-le-Vicomte's main defenders were members of the 17th SS Panzergrenadier Division Goetz von Berlichingen. They were an SS Waffen unit, made up of non-German volunteers (mostly Romanian and French in this case). The division was equipped with Sturmgeschuetz IVs, a Panzer IV modified as an assault gun or tank destroyer.

Well equipped, well trained, and well led, the grenadiers were among the toughest fighters we faced. But a bit of luck and heavy

firepower softened Saint-Sauveur-le-Vicomte up before we attacked. An alert scout spotted a large group of Germans retreating in the area, using the road through the village. A massive,
coordinated artillery barrage devastated them—and laid waste to
a lot of the town.

There were still German defenders, though, when Company F
arrived along the main road, within sight of a bridge leading to
the eastern part of town. Germans on a hill overlooking the road
opened up with artillery. With no cover, the only thing to do was
to run for the bridge.

Somewhere in there, some P-47s decided they should take the
bridge out. Fortunately, they and most of the German artillery
shells missed.

The company reassembled on the western bank. Roadblocks
were set up to prevent Germans who were retreating from the
north from entering the village. Meanwhile, other units flooded
in. There was stiff fighting in the streets, with our light artillery
dueling with German flak guns pressed into service to fire at people. The guns fired quickly, with a distinctive sound, almost like
an angry sewing machine. This was very unlike the heavier thud
and crack of bigger guns, which came at longer intervals.

Around 2200 hours, two fresh battalions of the 508th Parachute Infantry Regiment arrived. Saint-Sauveur-le-Vicomte was
secured.

————————

The Germans used a variety of weapons against us in the bocage. Their Tiger tank (which came in several variations and
two different versions) is most famous. The heavier Panther tank
had reached Normandy shortly before the invasion and fought

in the bocage as well as in the Caen area. By most counts, the Germans had more Panzer IV medium tanks in the Normandy area when we landed than any other tank. A number of captured French Renault tanks had been put into service as well; though lighter than their German counterparts and usually considered inferior, these could be potent enemies, as we'd seen in Sainte-Mère-Église. The tanks were often scavenged to be used in fixed positions, where gun and turret were called torbuks, or as the basis for mobile antiaircraft batteries and tank destroyers.

As ferocious as the tanks could be, the weapon everyone was afraid of was the German 88, an artillery piece originally designed as an antiaircraft gun. The Germans soon found that they could use the gun to take out tanks; unlike many antiaircraft weapons, the barrel could be aimed horizontally to aim at a ground target. Mounted on a truck chassis, the gun could be easily transported to where it was needed. It was so famous that most any time soldiers came under attack from unseen artillery, they'd blame it on 88s, rather than, say, the standard German howitzer, the Immergrün ("Evergreen"), which was pretty deadly on its own. The Immergrün fired a 15 cm, 44 kg shell a little more than 14,500 yards—eight miles, so you'd never know what killed you.

German artillery shells came in different sizes and flavors, ranging from hand grenades and mortars to the 1,500-pound monsters lobbed by the Schwerer Gustav—fortunately never against me. The Gustav was the largest rifled artillery piece of the war. It could fire a seven-ton projectile thirty miles; only three were built as far as is known, and none were used against us in Normandy.

The shells that were fired were of different types, with different killing specialties. Anti-armor shells were shaped so that they could pierce the armor of a tank. A high-explosive shell was packed so that not only was the blast itself deadly, but the explosion ripped the shell casing into shrapnel, which could be worse.

———————

The attack in the American sector went far better than in the British sector. Troops from our 9th Infantry Division reached the sea on June 19, cutting off the Cotentin Peninsula. Montgomery's offensive, though, stalled because of the defenses around Caen. That presented a new problem—if we kept going ahead, we might expose our own flank to a German counterattack. At the same time, we had not taken Cherbourg. General Bradley reshuffled his plans, stopping short of Saint-Lô and putting more men into the drive against Cherbourg.

The 82nd Airborne and our sister division, the 101st, remained in action, fighting now on the front lines rather than behind the lines, the way regular infantry would.

For me and the men I was with, that mostly meant we plodded through farm fields and small villages, taking on well-placed defenders. We might have outnumbered them, but they had the advantage of being on defense in a place where it was hard to maneuver.

If you looked at what was happening on a battle map, there would be large arrows sweeping this way and that. On the ground, it was men charging onto a hedgerow under heavy fire, fighting for maybe hours until enough of the enemy had been killed that the living gave up their positions and fell back. The victors would rush to the hedgerow, only to find that the Germans had been reinforced by defenders in the field where they had retreated. Then the process would start all over again.

Taking a city or village was no easier. The stone buildings made for easy cover; narrow streets were built for ambushes. The battle lines were also a lot more fluid than you might guess looking at that battle map. There were countless times when a unit would reach a certain spot along a road, then find Germans driving through a few moments later. While this occasionally made for some easy ambushes, it also meant that it was never possible to feel completely secure.

"WILL I BE AT PEACE?"

This one time we were coming out of an apple orchard to assault a building at the edge of a village. We had about, oh, fifty yards of open field between the trees and the building. We started across the field. Boy, the bullets started flying everywhere. Mortars started in as well.

A German machine gunner opened up. One of my friends, John, went down.

I couldn't stop.

I got into the house; I must have been one of the first inside. As I went into the hall, there was an explosion—someone in the squad had thrown a grenade through a window.

I was slammed to the ground.

My head blanked for a moment. I had only one thought:

I'm going to die.

But I was lucky. I didn't lose consciousness. I wasn't even hurt. The only thing I got out of that was a loud ringing in the ears. The thick walls had protected me. I got up and ran through; someone else had found the machine gunner.

Back outside, I went over to where John had fallen. He was badly wounded, bleeding; it was pretty clear he wasn't going to survive more than a few more minutes.

He somehow seemed calm, though. I'd seen several men die by this point, and the faces of many more who had died before I got there. They'd always had a look of agony on their faces, or an expression of surprise.

Not John. He was saying something. I bent and held him in my arms.

"Our Father, who art in Heaven, Hallowed be thy name . . ."

It was the Lord's Prayer, which I must confess I wasn't very familiar with at the time. What struck me wasn't the words so much as the look on his face.

He seemed at peace.

I couldn't make sense of that. It just seemed strange that he could be so calm when faced with dying. He passed a few minutes later.

Not many days after that, we were in a field bordered by a hedgerow. Another soldier, Bill, and I crossed into the vegetation. Bullets ripped through, and a mortar round maybe. He stumbled. I kept going; he didn't.

We fought to the other end of the field, finally chasing the Germans back. Low on ammo, I went to scavenge some and found Bill on the ground. He was dying.

I bent to him. He began saying something. Again, I didn't really recognize it, but pieces stayed with me. Later I found it was from Psalm 23: *The Lord is my shepherd . . .*

He, too, had that peaceful look.

As I've said, I didn't have religion during the war; if I wasn't an actual atheist, I was pretty close. But the memories of those two men remained with me throughout the rest of the war. It wasn't their faith at that point that impressed me. It was more a question:

Will I face death so calmly?

At that point, the answer certainly would have been no.

Yet death was all around me. Our guys, Germans. How many people I saw die, how many even I held just before they died—more than I can count now. By the end of the war the number was probably in the hundreds if not way beyond.

Could I face death as calmly as those two men had?

———————

Death sometimes grazed by me without me even noticing.

I was running for cover in one of those fields where the Germans had positioned a tank. One of our soldiers got close and managed to pop a grenade right into the open hatchway, blowing up the tank crew and the commander who was in the open turret.

Running forward, my helmet flew off; I had to go back for it when things calmed down.

There was a crease a half-inch in across the temple area.

My helmet hadn't fallen; it had been shot off.

WHAT WE SHARED

———————

Replacements for the men who were killed started coming in a few days after D-Day.

"What do we do?" they'd ask.

"Follow us," we'd tell them. "Keep your butt down."

And keep moving. That we learned real quick. You don't stop when you're fighting the Germans. Keep moving.

Shared danger built a bond between myself and the guys I'd work with; we were all "buddies," to use the word we used. New guys, old guys—all buddies. You didn't know the guy next to you, but if he was there, he was automatically a buddy.

There were people from places I'd never heard of. City guys and farm guys. The guys I met from New York, Chicago, Detroit, and all these other bigger cities, they were all good guys. Farm guys, too. People from the South. We had things in common besides the war. We all said the same thing:

When the war is over . . .

The words that followed differed from man to man, but the basic idea was the same:

I'm living for tomorrow, once I get through today.

But the plans weren't elaborate. Vague hopes, more like. We couldn't waste time figuring out tomorrow. We knew what was happening today and that's the way we lived for those few weeks. There was no future, except when it came. Which we all hoped it would.

Another thing: when you are a lowly private, you don't get that much information.

You're told to do things. Rarely are you told why. And never, or hardly ever, are you told where that *why* fits into the overall strategy.

That encourages living in the present, doing what has to be done to get to the next day, then the next, until finally the war is over and your future resumes.

I had Arlene's picture with me to remind me that there was a future. I looked at it every so often. I don't think I would have forgotten what she looked like, let alone forgotten her, but it was a good thing to have. A good thing to see.

V-1S AND NATURE'S RAVAGES

While our armies continued to advance, Hitler unleashed a frightening new weapon against the British, the V-1 or *Vergeltungswaffen-1*. Meant as retaliation for Allied bombing of German cities, there was no attempt at disguising what its purpose was: *Vergeltungswaffen* means "vengeance weapon."

Revenge.

For a war the Germans had started. Pretty perverted logic.

Developing the weapon, the Germans abandoned proposals that would have made it useful against specific military targets. The V-1 was intended solely as a weapon of mass destruction, striking at civilians.

The missiles began flying from the Pas-de-Calais region beginning on June 13.

Called "Buzz Bombs" because of the sound they made as they flew, these weapons were powered by a pulse-jet engine mounted about the tail end. Needle-nosed and stubby-winged, they were flown by a primitive autopilot that checked altitude and (in effect) distance flown. Once the predetermined distance was reached, the guidance system put the bomb into a sharp dive to the ground.

The warhead contained 1,000 kilograms (about 2,200 pounds) of amatol, a combination of TNT and aluminum nitrate, a common ingredient in bombs during the war. The weapons detonated on contact.

Germany launched more than nine thousand rockets; over six thousand civilians were killed and nearly eighteen thousand injured. Driving across the Cotentin Peninsula and then onward toward Cherbourg, American troops discovered missile and V-1 launching areas. They also discovered a more potent weapon, the

V-2 rocket, which had not yet been put into action. But there were
plenty more V-1s and V-2s in northern France, and the attacks
continued until the launching areas close enough to put London
in jeopardy were in Allied control. Even then, the Germans used
some against civilians in Belgium.

While they did not immediately affect those of us in Normandy, the vengeance weapons killed many civilians and eventually influenced Eisenhower's plans for conducting the war. They
also tied up fighters and antiaircraft weapons, and had a massive
psychological effect on the people living under their shadow.

The Allies had targeted Cherbourg at the top of the Cotentin
Peninsula so we'd have a port to supply our troops through. But
realizing that the city would not be taken quickly, the planners
had arranged to set up two artificial ports, one on Omaha and
the other on Gold. Known as Mulberries A (Omaha) and B (Gold),
they looked like extremely long piers jutting into the sea. Concrete caissons were set into the water; decking was attached
above. Breakwaters—more caissons and sunken ships—were arranged to give some shelter to the docks.

The Mulberries were a brilliant idea, but they were undone by
Mother Nature.

A huge storm hit the area June 19; it hung around for the next
two days. Inland, we were drenched. On the beaches, the gale-
force winds and driven rains shut down many operations. The
Mulberries were severely battered. Things were so bad at Omaha
that a few days after the storm passed, command decided to aban-
don the artificial harbor all together. Parts that could be salvaged
were sent over to the Mulberry at Gold.

The loss of Mulberry A hampered supply, especially for the American troops. While the Army scrambled to improvise, the campaign on the Cotentin Peninsula became even more important. We needed to take Cherbourg, and we needed to do it *now*.

While we were part of the force holding the line against German reinforcements and counterattacks, most of the 4th, 9th, and 79th Infantry Divisions with tank and artillery support marched on Cherbourg. Out in the English Channel, the Navy lined up a squadron of battleships and cruisers to pummel the city's defenses. Three battleships, four cruisers, and a handful of destroyers began turning the city into dust.

The bulk of the German troops left inside the city were members of the 709th Division. Though overmatched in manpower and arms, they held the city bitterly. Their commander, Generalleutnant Karl-Wilhelm von Schlieben, recognized that the situation was hopeless; with no way out, he asked for permission to surrender his troops.

Rommel told him to fight to the last bullet.

The Germans did almost that. The sea bombardment started June 25. The Americans fought nearly hand-to-hand in some of the city streets, making slow headway. Prisoners were taken—but most were Russian POWs who had agreed to fight for the Germans in exchange for not being killed or interred in prisoner of war camps.

Cornered in a tiny section of the city with a little under a thousand starving and almost ammo-less troops, von Schlieben finally disobeyed orders and surrendered on June 26; the last Germans at the port held out until the twenty-ninth. But the American troops arriving at the wharfs discovered that the Germans had sabotaged everything. In fact, they did such a good job—and booby-trapped so much of what was left—that it took many months to get the port facilities back in usable shape.

Cherbourg and the Cotentin Peninsula, won at such a huge cost of lives, never played the role in the war that the planners had hoped when designing D-Day.

───────────

Journalist Ernie Pyle, who became famous during the war for his on-the-spot reporting, was with the 4th Division as it moved against Cherbourg. Recounting a battle with troops fighting Germans they couldn't see in the outskirts of Cherbourg, Pyle wrote, "They were American boys who by mere chance of fate had wound up with guns in their hands, sneaking up a death-laden street in a strange and shattered city in a faraway country in a driving rain. They were afraid, but it was beyond their power to quit."

Pyle could have been writing about us all.

"IS THIS WHERE I DIE?"

───────────

We knew things were going well because we were pushing the Germans back. But we took a lot of losses, every time we took a hamlet or a hedgerow. It seemed like a never-ending thing. Some of the hedgerows were like mazes. I heard of some guys getting split up from their units and getting lost—not surprising.

Every day was a battle.

One time while we were in the hedgerows, we bypassed a German who was hiding in a trench in the undergrowth. Once I was behind him, I snuck back to shoot him, but my gun jammed. I took the jump knife from my boot, got close, and jumped at him, aiming to get my knife across his throat.

The knife killed him.

I was lucky he hadn't heard me get close, and didn't have his gun ready. I was lucky he was looking in the wrong direction, and didn't realize we'd gone by him.

I was lucky I'd had the training to do what had to be done. I could go on—let's just say I was lucky, and leave it at that.

The Thompson was a good weapon, but it would jam. It happened a couple of times to me. The ammunition wasn't perfect, and every so often, a bullet would hang up. Clearing it out wasn't a big deal—unless you were in the middle of a battle.

Which was the only time it would jam.

Those days were hard, but they blur together now. The times my friends were killed, the time a buddy threw a grenade in a tank, the time I got my helmet shot off—it all runs together.

It was like going to work the same old job every day, only this was one with bullets.

And no showers in the morning. Dinner with the family, though—the men you are with, whether you know them or not, are your family.

———————

It seemed to rain nearly every day during the last half of June. When it didn't rain, the sky was overcast and gray. Your uniform would be wet, boots soaked.

The 82nd and its regiments regrouped and probed German de-

fenses south of the Douve. There were definitely German strong-
points to our south; they would have to be destroyed for the Army
to move south into France. Patton's Third Army was scheduled to
land on the peninsula within a few days, once the way was cleared
for them. They were to strike south and east, while First Army,
which the airborne units were attached to, would head west.

I didn't know about those plans. I knew only what was in front
of me, which was more bocage.

On June 29, we were south of Saint-Sauveur-le-Vicomte, still in
the bocage country, though my memory is that the hedgerows
were not as thick in our immediate area. The weather that week
was dismal. A lot of rain and overcast skies.

We had pushed the Germans out of a field and moved up to another set of hedgerows. There were forty or fifty of us, all light arms.

One of the things that always happened, or seemed to—we'd
push them out of one set of hedgerows, and then get counterattacked from the next. Falling back, they'd regroup with defenders
and come at us again.

This day, we dug in, knowing that we weren't going to get any
farther for the moment.

Sure enough, the Germans counterattacked, I think around
3 P.M. They came back at us with three tanks, along with grenadiers moving with the tanks.

We could take care of the infantry no problem, but the armor
was a different story. I looked around for the bazooka man, hop-
ing he'd take one of the tanks. I finally saw him about twenty
yards behind me. He'd been knocked down by gunfire.

I got up, thinking I was going to grab the bazooka.

The rest was like a dream.

I glanced back and saw the tank—a German Tiger tank. Thick,

bulky front, massive gun in the turret. A gun so big it looked like it took up the whole top wedge of the tank. Ferocious muzzle at the end of the barrel.

Pointing straight at me.

The turret.

I thought, My God, he ain't going to shoot at me with that big gun.

But he did.

The shell landed behind me and our bazooka operator. I heard a tremendous clap, then nothing for a long, long time.

SIX

Prisoner

RECOVERY

I came to on a litter hours later, being carried by a German sergeant to some sort of aid station.

I was a prisoner of war. The Germans must have run our guys back a ways, then taken me off the battlefield with their own wounded.

The sergeant looked down at my dog tags after setting me down.

"You're German," he told me, in perfect English. "You shouldn't be fighting us."

I blanked out again.

The Germans put me in a truck that night with a couple of wounded soldiers. A medical aide or soldier pressed into that duty told me we were being taken to a field hospital to be patched up. He complained about our aircraft, which were harassing the Germans pretty good.

"They keep shooting our trucks up, your doggone planes. We're taking you at night so there's no danger of strafing."

He, too, was speaking English. It was surprising how many Germans did.

The more incredible thing was how much pain I was in. Like being on fire and being squeezed by giant claws and being pulled apart, all at the same time. My back and legs hurt most—I found out later I'd taken shrapnel there—but the pain had no real barriers. Everything hurt.

I went in and out of consciousness. Every so often the truck hit some massive pothole or bump and the shock wave spit through my body and shook my brain awake. I'd sink back to black darkness, only to be shocked back to painful awareness again.

Finally, I settled into a static state, gone mentally, aware only of the pain.

When I came to, I was in a field hospital. A doctor told me that he had done some minor work, apparently taking some shrapnel from my leg and back, but that I needed more serious surgery. Whatever it was, they weren't able to take care of it there.

They bandaged me up. This time they put some drugs in me that took the edge off the pain, and helped me sleep—not peacefully, but with less interruption. Later that night, we moved out again, this time by truck and then train, heading toward Paris, deep behind enemy lines.

———

The irony is, the 82nd Airborne Division was moved out of Normandy two weeks later, returning to England for refitting.

I missed freedom by that much.

But that would be true for a lot of guys. One more battle, one more bullet, a day, a week.

———————

The trip to the German hospital took a night. Once more I was operated on. Once more the doctor who met me afterward spoke perfect English.

His first words had nothing to do with the surgery.

"You were lucky," he said. "The train behind you was shot up by your own people."

I guess luck is always a matter of perspective.

The tank I'd seen hadn't hit me point blank, if it even fired at all. Whatever had exploded nearby and knocked me out had sent shrapnel into my legs and back. The doctor explained, briefly, that the wounds in my legs weren't that bad. My back would be okay as well, but they had to leave some of the shrapnel there. It was too deep to get without risking injury to my spine. As long as the metal didn't move around too much, it wouldn't be a problem.

I'd be able to walk with it, he told me. "Just don't mess with it."

I wasn't about to.

That was luck, too, I suppose—hit in the back, but still able to walk. Knocked out, but still alive. A prisoner, but in a hospital.

Somehow, none of that made me feel very lucky.

"You're out of the war for sure now," the doctor added before he left. "Good luck. I hope you make it home."

I was in the Paris hospital about a month. I remember a few British soldiers were there, and maybe an American or two, but the Germans were very careful to keep us apart from one another.

Most of the wounded were German soldiers, who of course had few kind words for me.

The French orderlies and nurses, on the other hand, treated me like a king. They made sure I had a cold glass of water when I was thirsty—a true treat. They made sure I got food, which was something that could be quite random, even among the wounded Germans I was in with.

Cold water and regular meals were luxuries. I guess that says a lot about war and where I was.

A couple of the nurses could speak English. If the Germans weren't around, they might whisper something about the war, telling me that the Allies were moving closer. They'd mention a town. I would have no idea where that town was. I just knew it sounded positive.

"We're so glad you Americans are here," they'd say, careful to make sure they couldn't be overheard.

Arlene was at work in the machine-gun factory when she got a phone call from my mother.

"The Army—they told us . . ." My mother couldn't get the words out. "Henry is missing. He's missing."

Arlene and her mom left work to go home and pray.

CATTLE CARS

After a few weeks, the Germans decided I was in good enough health to be taken to a prison camp. They loaded me with other prisoners on a boxcar. A "forty and eight," the French called them.

They'd been designed to hold forty men or eight horses. There were little windows toward the top, like open slats to let air in. They were closed off by barbed wire.

They were cattle cars to me, old, rancid-smelling boxcars packed real tight with prisoners. The prisoners were mostly Brits and Poles, with one or two Americans besides myself. I'm guessing many like me had been fighting in Normandy on D-Day or soon afterward, and then captured. They hadn't been with me in the hospital, so they must have been at other hospitals or maybe camps nearby. With the Allies pressing in, perhaps the Germans were taking everyone east.

We were in so tight, not everyone could sit down. The stronger guys took turns standing so the men who were pretty weak could rest.

"Stronger" was a comparative term.

The Germans didn't give us any food or water when we left. It was two days before we got anything, and that was water shot from a hose through some of those windows. You had to catch it with your mouth. We'd clump together near the window, openmouthed like baby birds begging for something from their mother. You'd get a few drops, if you were lucky, then maybe sidle away so someone else could "drink."

Then we'd ride again.

Imagine the urine in that car after only a day.

Imagine everything else.

The train traveled at night. I'm not sure how long we were in the cars or how far they actually went. The train tracks in France and Germany had been bombed so badly that all the trains had to take very indirect routes. You go ninety miles to get to a place that before the war was only ten miles of track away.

THE DEATH CAMP

The train would make stops at sidings, maybe to get more fuel or avoid other trains. We did this for several days—a week, less, more, I'm not certain. One day we heard explosions and the drone of many aircraft. We were near a city that must have been targeted for a bombing attack. The train pulled to a stop; there was a commotion outside—the guards apparently were running for shelter, leaving the locked boxcars and train behind.

Within a few minutes, the drone of the airplanes grew louder. Explosions and gunfire—everyone in the car tried to shrink into the tiniest space possible. There were shrieks, and loud rattles, then nothing.

Eventually the guards came back. We were let out of the boxcar, into a barbed-wire and fenced-off area directly behind the tracks.

The two cars after us in the train had been shot up badly. Bodies were being taken off; apparently they'd been shot up in the attack. We guessed that an American fighter plane or fighters had escorted the bombers nearby and come down to do a little freelancing, not knowing his target was actually filled with Allied POWs.

Just a guess.

An even deeper horror sat on the other side of the fence where we were imprisoned: piles of dead bodies, rotting in the open air.

We'd pulled into a death camp.

I don't know about the others, but I had never heard about concentration camps, and had no idea what I was seeing. It was a horror beyond my understanding. Not long after, another train arrived, this one on a different siding or some track we couldn't see. We heard guards shouting, and caught glimpses of people being marched inside the complex.

Later, wooden carts brought out more bodies to be stacked up near the fence.

We were in that yard about a week. The dead bodies were moved away—maybe burned. The whole time I wondered when we would be next. Questions circled in my head.

Are they just waiting for room for us?

Why don't they just kill us and get it over with?

There were children there, weren't there? And women? Why are they being killed? How?

No answers. I just kept waiting to die on the other side of that wire.

———————

The train was moved away after a day or two, leaving us penned in by the rolled wire and fence. I could see now that four cars had been shot up. Other trains came in, filled with people, continuing the horrible routine: shouted commands, walking, death. We remained in our enclosure, guarded, next to the dead bodies, watching the piles grow and then diminish.

It was hot, and between the dead and ourselves, the place must have stunk. But I lost my sense of smell. Or the memory of the stench is so horrible my brain has wiped it away.

We were fortunate that the weather hadn't turned cold yet. We had only the clothes on our backs to keep us warm. It rained once or twice; we had to put up with that. We slept on the ground, worn out from everything. You'd curl up wherever you were, maybe your arm for a pillow.

The guards treated us like vermin. Take a step out of line and you'd get whacked with a rifle butt.

I avoided that. Mostly I kept to myself. There may have been two or three other Americans in the fifty or so men I was imprisoned with, but I barely spoke to them or anyone. I was numb, in a kind of shock, certain I was going to die and unsure how I would act when the moment came.

Resigned, maybe. Defeated.

All those dead bodies near the fence. Was there a look of peace in anyone's eyes, or horror?

What would I have seen if I looked in a mirror? Horror, I'm sure.

There was some food. Sugar beet soup, probably made from scraps, and ersatz bread—ersatz because a good part of it was actually sawdust instead of flour.

———————

It took about a week before repairs to the damaged train lines were made. A new train came in and we were moved again.

I guess we were happy not to have been killed there. We were so worn down and exhausted by then, and sickened by what we'd seen, that the word "happy" really doesn't describe our feelings. We'd survived, and there was a bit of relief in that.

Maybe that's a better word. "Relieved."

Relieved at having survived. Anxious about what was coming next.

———————

For years I've thought the camp we were parked in was Auschwitz, the large concentration and extermination camp the Germans operated in occupied Poland.

Someone in the Army said that based on some information that they had, and I never really questioned it. I knew nothing of the camps when I joined the Army, and didn't know anything about them before the war, only afterward. What I saw on the other side of that wire certainly seemed horrible enough to be Auschwitz, probably the most notorious of the many concentration camps run by the Third Reich.

The massive camp included Birkenau and many satellite camps, places of horror and unbelievable atrocities. It is estimated that a million Jews were murdered there, most by poison gas soon after they arrived. Those who weren't killed outright were put to work, which is another way of saying that the Germans killed them by working them to death. Or tried to; the war ended before they succeeded in every case.

Auschwitz is in Poland, which is a long way from where I was captured. In researching this book, we came to a tentative conclusion that the camp I was parked in probably wasn't in Poland; more likely it was a death camp in or near southern Germany or Czechoslovakia. Auschwitz can't be completely ruled out, however. We simply don't know now why the person who said Auschwitz thought that; we've been unable to find records that might prove it, or disprove it for that matter. In fact, it's impossible to completely rule out any of the camps.

In a way, it doesn't matter. The horrors I saw were repeated in death camps throughout occupied Europe. I doubt the address made any difference to the poor souls who were tortured and killed there.

The evil I saw was beyond words. It seemed something only nonhuman beasts would be capable of.

But humans did it. The Germans did it. As difficult as it was to believe that, no denial was possible.

THE STALAG

The train traveled for another few days, until finally one day after we stopped, six guards arrived at the side of it. They pulled open the doors to our car and yelled at us to get out. Waving machine guns at us, they formed us into a line.

Raus!

They led us inside to the camp, fed us, and put us in a barracks.

We soon learned that this was a processing center rather than a regular camp, and we'd be assigned a permanent "residence." We were given POW tags and told we would be shipped out again.

That happened a few days later. Packed on the train car, crammed as before, I stood and sometimes sat over the next day and maybe night—it was dark in the car; I lost track—as we trundled across more countryside, ducking Allied planes. By now hunger was just another part of you, along with the aches and pains, something you wore like your soiled clothes.

The camp we were taken to had the look of a factory complex gone downhill and turned into a prison. There was one large building, and smaller ones that had been turned into barracks. Two fences and barbed wire surrounded the yard; guards in towers with machine guns stood over the fences. Dog handlers patrolled the perimeter. The outer fence had warning signs that said it was electrified; whether that was true or not, no one ever tested it.

We were marched into a large central area and made to stand at attention. A German officer with a deep, stern frown came out and scolded us in English.

"I am the commandant," he said, speaking English with a strong but understandable accent. "You are here as prisoners of war. You will work. If you don't work, the alternative is not good."

He said some other things, then this:

"If you think you're going to escape, I'll tell you right now that if you escape, we always catch you. We will bring you back and we'll shoot you."

That turned out to be the most accurate thing any German officer ever said to me.

Paratroopers in the 82nd Airborne Division prepare to go out on D-Day.

Two C-47 Skytrains, similar to the plane I jumped from in the early morning of D-Day.

A photo of me in uniform, before going off to Europe.

Arlene, the love of my life, whom I met a few months before joining the Army. She waited for me throughout the war.

"I'M CONSERVING WOOL, THIS BATHING SUIT'S PAINTED ON".

A World War II–era cartoon about rationing.

PLEASE DRIVE CAREFULLY, MY BUMPERS ARE ON THE SCRAP HEAP

Stars like Rita Hayworth, shown here, helped raise awareness about recycling metal—even car bumpers.

Even with rationing, there were often long lines for items like sugar, as this photo from New York shows.

C-47 Skytrains in action.

May 27, 1944

Dearest Mom & Dad

I'm sorry this is the first chance I have had to write this week I have been pretty busy. I have a quite a bit of washing to do to marrow so I shall be busy most of the day Sunday is as work to day here as well as any place else. "Say" mom I meant to ask you in my other letter wether you have recieved my $80 or not I sent it about two or three weeks ago so write and let me know if you recieved it please?

The last letter I would write my parents during the war.
Dated May 27, 1944, ten days before my jump, it tells of the mundane
details of army life and asks after my parents' garden.

General Dwight D. Eisenhower giving his famous pep talk
to troops before the invasion of Normandy.

General James Gavin
(left) of the 82nd
Airborne, with Field
Marshal Bernard
Montgomery.

A group of paratroopers from the 82nd head for their plane during maneuvers just prior to D-Day. Our seemingly endless practice sessions prepared us for much of what we encountered.

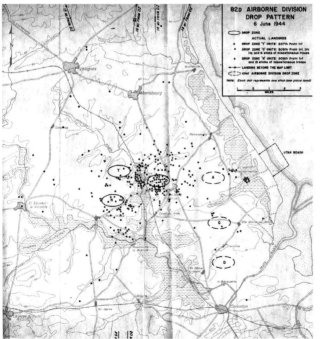

Where 82nd Airborne troopers landed on D-Day.

A 1944 photo of the village of Sainte-Mère-Église, where I crash-landed on June 6.

Our ultimate goal on D-Day was to protect the troops landing
on Utah Beach. While their battle wasn't nearly as bad as what happened
on Omaha, things could easily have gone poorly for them if we'd failed.
This photo shows the landing early on, still opposed but gaining steam.

The village of Sainte-Mère-Église remembers the 82nd in many ways, including with this likeness of John Steele caught on the roof of the church.

Members of the 82nd donated a stained glass window in the church to honor the events of that day.

La Fiere today, with its bridge still standing.

La Fiere, as seen from above.

A plaque commemorating the battle that took place there.

THE BATTLE FOR LA FIERE BRIDGEHEAD 6 - 9 JUNE 1944

The area encompassing both the La Fiere bridge and the causeway with the sister bridge and causeway at Chef du Pont were crucial objectives for this portion of the Normandy invasion. From 6 to 9 June the battle raged within sight of this monument. As a final " all in " assault at 10h30 on 9 June the causeway and bridgehead at Cauquigny church were seized by elements of the 82nd Airborne Division supported by elements of the 4th and 90th Infantry Divisions and the 746th Tank Battalion.

For the Normandy campaign the 82nd Airborne awarded an estimated

38 Distinguished Service Crosses
271 Silver Stars
925 Bronze Stars
5,209 Purple Hearts

Two Medals of Honor were awarded for actions within sight of this monument.

PRIMARY UNITS ENGAGED WITHIN SIGHT OF THIS LOCATION:

1st Bn 505th PIR
507th PIR
508th PIR
G/3-325th GIR / 2nd Bn 401st GIR
325th GIR (-)
307th Abn Engr Bn
80th AAA Bn (Anti-tank)
Command Group 82nd Airborne Div

APPROXIMATE CASUALTIES AT AND NEAR THIS LOCATION :

Killed 254   Wounded 525

"One of the most hotly contested pieces of ground in WW2"
(SLA Marshall - US Army historian)

THE SOUL OF THE AIRBORNE RESIDES IN THIS PLACE

7 juin 2015   Association AVA

Hedgerows in the French countryside. Many were taller than I was.

INSCRIPTIONS

HOMMES 40
CHEVAUX (EN LONG) 8

A forty-and-eight, much like the one that transported me to a prison camp. These are British troops in happier days before Germany took over France.

An SS propaganda photograph of Volkssturm and other Germans.
Most were older men, no longer fit for frontline duty.

DEUTSCHER VOLKSSTURM
WEHRMACHT

An armband with the insignia of the group I grew to hate.

A photograph of Arlene and my Bible, two items that helped me make it through the war.

The gun I took from the man who killed my friend.

While I was a POW, the Allies pressed eastward. The next big air operation was in the Netherlands during Operation MarketGarden.

The end of the war: On January 12, 1946, the 82nd Airborne led a parade through New York City.

With President Nicolas Sarkozy of France, who in 2007
honored me with the French Legion of Honor.

In uniform, at home in Clinton, Iowa.

———
———

SEVEN

The Mines

I WON'T DO IT
———

Conditions at the camp weren't very good. The buildings were sparse, the bunks uncomfortable. The food was the same as we'd had before—weak beet soup, ersatz bread, a slice about two by two inches.

We were kept in one area of the camp, separated from other prisoners and their barracks by barbed wire and guards. There were a lot more men there—a few hundred, maybe a thousand.

There were two to four other Americans in my section, out of thirty or forty total. The others were a sprinkling of Brits, Czechs, and Russians. Guards stayed with us in the barracks, and we weren't supposed to talk to each other.

The guards who worked at the camp and the mines were from two different organizations, judging from their uniforms, and to a point their attitude. The ones who ran the camp seemed to be either regular soldiers or maybe an auxiliary or Volkssturm, home guards, a militia formed to relieve regular soldiers for frontline duty. The others, who were in charge of the mine but were also at the camp, wore black uniforms with skull insignias—SS men.

The guards in the barracks were mostly older men. They weren't nice, but they were a sight better than the SS, who always accompanied us when we were working and were cruel beyond reason.

Not too long after I arrived, we were called out into one of the courtyards. There was a brick wall at one end, and it didn't take too much imagination to realize this was used as an execution space. Two long, rectangular boxes sat against the wall. The prisoners were marched past them. Inside the boxes were the bodies of two Russians, shot after being captured following an attempted escape.

"That is what happens when you escape," the commandant told us. His tone was anything but remorseful.

———————————

I'd been at the camp maybe a day or two when we were called out to go to work in the nearby coal mines. Thirty of us were formed into a line and marched out the camp gate and through the woods. I just followed along, trying to understand exactly what I was doing and what was going on. Different emotions fought inside me: anger, hatred, fear. The memory of the death camp was vivid. I didn't want to die, and yet I felt I had to fight the insane evil all around me.

Strong forces: Preservation. Revenge.

Surviving the effects of either is difficult; to deal with both at the same time—and with many others—might be impossible. Especially if you are not yet twenty-one.

We went down into the mine. I was assigned a cart to load. It was a small mining car on a track; it would be filled with coal, then moved out of the shaft and back up to a collection point.

"That's against the Geneva Convention," I said. "Working for the war effort."

The SS guard who'd taken me there knocked me down and worked me over.

I didn't work that day.

The next day, same thing.

Shnell!

No, I said. I told you yesterday, that's against the Geneva Convention.

He worked me over even harder that day.

As I lay on the ground, a little Czech man came over to me and in broken English told me if I didn't work, they'd just kill me.

My ribs said the same thing. They were probably broken.

The man told me that his partner had been sick the day before and been carried away; now he was gone—dead, I'd guess. I didn't realize it at the time, but this was the Czech's way of telling me that I was going to be his partner, and he would look after me, to the extent that was possible in this hellhole.

I didn't work that day, and barely was able to march back to camp. American bombers—you could tell they were ours by the heavy drone of the four-engined aircraft—hit the nearby area the next day. That was fortunate for me, since it meant that we didn't go to the mines, and I was able to recuperate a bit more.

The next day, assembling and marching back, I decided that if I was going to survive, I was going to work. There was no other choice.

So I did.

I had never seen a mine before. I knew nothing about how they worked, aside from the fact that they were underground. I was about to find out a lot more than I ever wished I knew.

The mine shaft where we worked must have been a quarter mile down. A few prisoners would get aboard a metal-floor elevator and wait as it slowly descended. When it reached the bottom of the shaft, we'd be let into a passage maybe fifteen or sixteen feet wide. From there we would walk down to "rooms" to mine soft brown coal.

I had the idea that the coal was being used to make electricity—something I was familiar with because of a similar plant back in Clinton. I'm not an expert on coal, then or now. As I understand it, there are four general grades, with different properties and uses. The coal here was very soft, a type called lignite. Because it doesn't give off that much heat when burned, it is considered a low grade and is most often used at power plants, where it can be turned into synthetic gas or burned on its own.

The shaft had overhead lights, strung at long intervals. The dreary shadows they cast looked bright compared to the rooms, which were lit only by the carbide lamps we carried. These rooms were shaped like the insides of igloos, the interior chipped away by successive shifts of workers. While the shaft roofs were supported by timbers, the rooms of coal had no supports.

When the coal ran out—or maybe before—the roofs would collapse. Experienced miners usually could tell when that was going to happen.

Not always.

They worked us in twelve-hour shifts, with twelve-hour breaks.

We had picks and shovels at the mine; you'd leave them, march back to the barracks, and collapse in a bunk that some other prisoner had slept in a short while before. We would alternate between night and day, spending about two weeks on one shift, then going to the other. The mines were somewhere between a mile and three away; it might take an hour to get there, depending on the weather. Coming back could take longer, depending on how tired we were.

Underground, you don't know whether it's day or night, so that doesn't really matter. The fatigue had built up in me pretty quick; the effects of changing work times was nothing compared to everything else.

My Czech friend looked as if he was sixty years old. I'd guess now, though, that he might have been half that. The work and poor food had stolen his years away. I asked him one time how long he'd been there.

Four years.

I gathered he was some sort of political prisoner. That took in a lot of possibilities. I never got any details.

The German guards seemed to respect him. Sometimes I thought he might be spying on the prisoners, and maybe getting better food or something in exchange. More likely, he'd just been there so long that he knew everything there was to know about the place and didn't give the guards trouble. Whatever the story was, he was very afraid of them. And he was certainly doing what he had to to survive.

Maybe a little more, in helping me.

My job, like the Czech's, like everyone's there, was to load a cart up with the coal. The carts would be taken down the shaft to an elevator and taken up. It was backbreaking and monotonous work. The guards would watch from the shaft area—they rarely went into the rooms—and never had a good word to say about what you were doing.

It was always, work harder. Faster. *Schnell, schnell.*

We'd go for six hours, then get a break for lunch or dinner or whatever they considered it. We'd sit on a bench in the shaft and eat more ersatz bread and soup. Then back to work.

There were accidents all the time. Rocks would tumble in abandoned rooms, sending smoke and dust into the tunnel and shifting the earth above us. We'd feel rumbling when they blasted new veins, and wonder if the entire mine might collapse. You never felt safe.

One day the old Czech guy and I went out of the room and sat next to each other on a bench a short distance away to eat. A few bites in, there was a terrible noise, and thick dust and smoke—the room we'd been in had just collapsed.

The old Czech just shook his head.

I'd learned my lesson about openly defying the guards, but I was still defiant. I thought about different ways to fight back. The only thing I could come up with was loading some rocks with the coal in the cart.

Maybe it would foul up their machinery. At least it was something.

I tossed a few rocks in with a load. I did it again, this time with more rocks. And again, with even more.

That afternoon, a guard came and asked if I knew what number my cart was.

"The cart has a number on it?" I asked.

"Yes, it's got a number on it."

I hadn't known.

"You've been putting rocks in with the coal," the guard said. "That's sabotage!"

Before I got a chance to deny it—I wouldn't have explained it, certainly—he gave me a smash. He worked me over pretty well with the butt of his rifle. When he was done, he looked at me and said, "If you do that again, you won't live to see the daylight out of this building."

I didn't do it again.

GENEVA CONVENTION

Let me first say this: in war, there really are no rules. Rules are things that aren't just agreed on, but can be enforced by an outside power, a referee or a justice system.

There was no referee in World War II. Each side held themselves to standards that they decided were fair; they were the judge and jury on that, at least until the war ended. Their consciences were their guide—except at times when their consciences collided with what was necessary to win the war.

Individuals on both sides committed atrocities, sometimes under the command of higher officers, sometimes not. That's not what I'm talking about here. Cruelty toward prisoners was a conscious policy among the Germans, certainly at that camp.

During World War II, prisoners were covered by the "Convention Relative to the Treatment of Prisoners of War. Geneva, 27 July 1929"—what we call the Geneva Convention. The document has ninety-seven articles, along with an annex. Among other things, it says POWs must be removed from the battlefield quickly, their countries notified. They must be treated with respect and some care.

POWs *could* be put to work—though not to do anything that directly benefited the war effort, which I believe mining that coal did. The conditions demanded by the Geneva Convention were a far cry from what we experienced.

And just for laughs, consider this: Article 28 says I should have been paid for my labor.

I wonder where I go to collect.

———————

One thing the Germans did that I guess would count as an act of kindness: they let me keep my Bible and my picture of Arlene.

"Pretty girl," said one of the officers who examined me before handing it back.

I used it as a bookmark, reading the Bible. I kept both in my breast pocket as I worked.

The guards in the mine were sadistic, and I'm not sure why they didn't take the picture or the Bible. They had their chance every day. One guard in particular enjoyed pointing at me and then running his finger across his throat before going out of the "opyo," as they called the rooms where we mined the coal. Maybe he was a Christian, and believed the Bible would help me toward salvation.

It may be that the officers thought it would make me more docile. Arlene's photo, though?

That one's a puzzler. Maybe they saw it as something that would remind me I had hope—and that therefore I should do what they say. Maybe they had sweethearts of their own, and took pity, such as it was.

———————

Each day in the mine, you had a quota: fill up four carts or be beaten. I didn't work quickly, but I did meet my quotas. Getting beaten made you weak—or I should say, weaker than you were. Getting weaker made it more possible you'd collapse. And collapsing made it likely you'd die.

Bodies were always being left at the tipple, the entrance to the mine. We'd see them every time we came up to go back to the barracks. What was once a human being was now trash for buzzards.

Sometime that winter, I began to get a bad chest cold. As the days went on, trudging back and forth between the cold and damp, alternately freezing and sweating and then freezing again, I came down with pneumonia.

I didn't know what I had, but I knew what I didn't have: energy. Tired and aching and hungry and cold, then hot, then cold, I trudged into the mines even so. Get sick and you were done.

One morning I had nothing, no energy, no will really. But I remembered what the Czech had told me in those first few days, about his sick friend who had disappeared. I said nothing.

As we worked, I slipped or something. The next thing I knew, I was being carried out. The Germans were taking me. It was the end.

To my surprise, I wasn't brought to a crematorium or stood up against a wall and shot. They put me in a small infirmary and let me recover there.

Within a few days, I was back in the mines, working as hard as ever.

DEATH, SLOW OR QUICK

Each day at the mine was marked by an unspoken ritual: the steady exhaustion of the workers.

Heavy physical labor for twelve hours, day after day, is bad enough. That labor without adequate food, under high stress and the constant threat of beatings, to say nothing of the injuries that had accompanied us here—it was a formula for death.

It wouldn't happen as quick as a bullet, maybe, but it would happen nonetheless. Every day when we came up from the mine, greeted by a body or two retrieved earlier, we knew that was our fate. The men we'd marched with had been worked to death. When would it happen to us?

I'd arrived in the fall, when the weather was still relatively warm. Now it was cold.

Christmas—did Christmas come? I can't say. Thanksgiving, of course, didn't. New Year's?

If they did, they passed without me knowing.

In America, a song from the movie *Meet Me in St. Louis* became an instant classic. Written by Hugh Martin and Ralph Blaine, the song was so bittersweet that Judy Garland, who was to sing it in the film, at first refused.

People would cry, she said. There was too much longing for

times that had passed, too much sadness, too much emphasis on current hard times and missing boys.

And this—words that said this Christmas "might be your last."

A few changes were made, though much of the bittersweet tone remained below the surface. "Have Yourself a Merry Little Christmas" became an instant classic.

———————

The weather gradually got worse, damp and cold. Down in the mine, you worked so hard you sweat. Then you'd come back up, and as you were marched back to camp your clothes would freeze on you.

I was still wearing my old uniform—it stayed with me right across Europe, shrapnel holes and all. That was my winter coat.

As the times passed, I made a friend at the camp. Jim. He'd been a paratrooper, too. He was about my age, maybe a little older. He was an American. He was worn down as I was.

That's all I really knew about him.

We saw each other on the way to and from the mine, some-times marching together. Back in the barracks, we would hang out together, as much as that was possible when you were ex-hausted from a full day's labor.

One day we got to talking about how death was inevitable. The Germans were working us into our graves.

We were going to die. It was just a question of when.

There was no hope in escape. Everyone who tried was brought back dead.

Still, that was a choice, wasn't it? To try to escape was at least defiance. Even with no hope, it was at least action. It meant taking your life in your hands.

Foolishness. Surely the war would end soon. Surely someday we would be liberated.

The bodies kept appearing at the end of each shift. The war continued, endlessly, it seemed.

How did we want death, slow or quick?

====================

EIGHT

The War Outside the Fence

MIA

In early October, my father got a letter from the War Department:

Dear Mr. Langrehr:

As promised you, I am writing again regarding your son, Private First Class Henry O. Langrehr. . . .

   It has been my fervent hope that favorable information would be forthcoming and that you might be relieved from the great anxiety which you have borne during these months. It is therefore with deep regret that I must state that no further report in his case has been forwarded to the War Department.

   I want to again emphasize the fact that the Commanding Generals in all our theaters of Operations are making a continuous effort to establish the actual status of personnel who have been reported as missing, or missing in action. In many instances the War De-

partment must rely upon the reports by a belligerent government through the International Red Cross for information.

You may be certain that when any information is received, it will be promptly transmitted to you. In the event no additional information is received within the next three months, I will again communicate with you.

Sincerely yours,

J. A. Ulio
Major General,
The Adjutant General.

I can't imagine how Arlene would have felt when she heard the news.

Helpless?

Angry?

Baffled?

Yet always when asked about me being MIA, she replied simply that she was sure I was still alive, and would be home soon.

Arlene was still working with her mother at the local factory making the stands for machine guns. As long as the days were, Arlene was proud to be doing something for the war effort. Sometimes I think she was superhuman, doing all that; she just smiles when someone mentions the amount of work or strain. It wasn't so unusual; people at home wanted to do something that contributed to the war effort.

There were other reasons. Money was one; the factories were paying well. Others had to do with wishing the war would be over quickly, and maybe helping that come true. Some were patriotism, and national spirit. And there was a feeling of being in it together, working hard side by side with other people doing the same.

The home front was not a perfect place; evil didn't suddenly disappear. There would be plenty of investigations later into war profiteering that had hurt soldiers while enriching a few. Still, the overall feeling among most people was one of cooperation and pulling together for the good of the country.

———————

Besides working hard, Arlene must also have been tempted by the young soldiers who passed through the hospital or town on business. I'd bet more than a few were better looking than me.

But she stayed true, just knowing that I was coming home.

I've asked her about it many times since, looking maybe for some magic formula or a hidden knowledge. Her answer has always been the same:

I just knew.

She prayed, and she went to church, but as important as her faith was to her, she just knew I was coming home no matter how many prayers she said or didn't. She could no more doubt that than she could forget her own name.

There must have been temptations galore. There were many local dances sponsored by different groups, and a lot of times for fun, Arlene and an aunt would go along to them. The two women would dance together, which was the custom if you didn't want to attract undue male attention. But the attractive young woman with the fashionable curl in her hair would still be asked by handsome bachelors if she wanted to take a turn with them; she always turned them down.

Rationing was in full effect. Items needed for the war effort were in very short supply, but the shortages included things you wouldn't think of—food, for example. Sugar and flour were important staples—but to get them, you needed coupons. If you lived on a farm or had enough land for a garden, then you grew and canned vegetables and fruit. Otherwise, canned goods were often the only thing you could find, and you generally needed coupons to buy them. Coffee, too. Gasoline and fuel oil for heating were limited as well.

The rules could be complex. There were "red foods" and "blue foods," which corresponded to the coupons that could be used to purchase each—assuming you could find them. If you stayed in a hospital for more than ten days, you had to turn your coupon book in. When someone died, the family's stamp allocation was reduced. In theory, families were issued coupons based on their needs, but that often didn't cover what you needed or at least wanted. Having a large family and a group of friends could help. Arlene and her family would trade or give coupons to each other to make up for shortfalls—even though it was against the rules.

Soup was a favorite meal. It stretched the small amount of meat, and it was versatile, since it could be made with whatever vegetables you had at hand.

Arlene's dad got gasoline coupons, but because his truck was old—it started with a hand crank, which even by 1940 would have made it long obsolete—he rarely drove it. He would give gasoline stamps he didn't need to others who did. Fortunately, the bus service in Clinton was very good.

Often, people who lived in town and around our county would just walk to where they needed to go. Arlene and her mother walked to work though it was a half-mile away, and thought nothing of walking even ten miles to see someone if the weather wasn't against them.

Recycling metals and even cooking fats was standard. Every tin can was potentially a munition—or so it was said.

The government started price controls to keep people from gouging, and to try to keep inflation down. That worked a bit, but prices always seemed to be rising. Black markets for goods sprung up around the country, where people would buy goods without coupons but with very high prices. If there were any in Clinton, though, our families didn't know about them—and they didn't have the money to spare, besides.

Arlene's father got a job in a local factory canning corn during the early days of the war. But something happened there—apparently someone took offense because he was German—and he quit and never went back. Instead, he ended up as an Electrolux salesman, going door-to-door hawking vacuums.

Sales were tough during the war. His wife would watch out the window when he came home, trying to guess from his stride if he'd sold anything that day—no sales, no pay.

As they grew older, Arlene's brothers joined the service, as did mine.

On the coasts, cities and towns had air raid drills, with varying degrees of success. Children went to school with tags on their clothes to identify themselves and their parents in case the worst happened. At night, wardens walked the streets yelling at people to put out their lights; they worried that they would guide German or Japanese bombers to a target.

The newspapers and radio stations carried information from the fronts. Much of the news was heavily censored, in an effort to keep from giving information to the enemy somehow. The most reliable thing in the papers were the lists of the dead.

MARKETGARDEN AND THE BULGE

A lot had happened in the war since my capture.

Hampered by German defenses and the unfamiliar terrain, our troops had bogged down in the bocage by early July. After several attempts at a breakthrough, First Army launched a massive offensive in the area of Saint-Lô. Obliterating frontline defenses with an innovative, massive bombing attack—strategic bombers were used as artillery would have—our guys broke through the German defenses. Troops poured down the Cotentin Peninsula, beginning a rout. General George Patton's Third Army, freshly arrived from Great Britain, joined in. The Germans were pummeled in a mass exodus from the Falaise Pocket. Paris was liberated by the French, with a great deal of American help, on August 24.

By then, a second front had been opened in France. Operation Dragoon launched the U.S. 7th Army into the area east of Marseille. The force leapt northward, striking toward the Rhone River and forcing the Germans back in the direction of the Black Forest and Rhine River.

By the end of August, our troops stood at the border of Germany. General Bradley argued for an assault across the border, aiming to punch quickly to Berlin. Backed by First Army general Courtney Hodges and Patton (Bradley as army group commander was their boss, but he worked closely with both), Bradley proposed a lightning strike that would hit Germany before the country could organize its defenses. He also suggested obliterating everything in their path, aiming to do to German civilians what their armies had imposed on the rest of the world.

Whatever effect that might have had, neither Bradley's suggestion nor his plan to cross into Germany was adopted.

———————

The 82nd Airborne had been moved out of the bocage and onto Utah Beach July 11. Seventeen LSTs—massive landing ships designed to move tanks—transported the division back to England.

That sounds like a lot, but in fact the unit had been drained of manpower. Before our jump, the 82nd's head count was roughly 11,770, all in—counting officers and enlisted, "regular" paratroopers, and all the men in the attached units.

About a tenth of the division—1,142—had been killed. Another 2,373 were wounded. And 840 were missing or captured.

I was one of them.

The 82nd had spent a little more than a month in combat. They spent the next two months refitting, filling their ranks with replacements for the lost men, and preparing for the next battle.

Which began September 17.

———————

Rather than following the plan Bradley and his lieutenants had proposed, Eisenhower endorsed a plan favored by Montgomery

code-named MarketGarden. In brief, the idea was to cross the
Rhine in the north, opening a way to Berlin. If successful, it would
get around the German defenses known as the Siegfried Line.
This was a massive series of defenses, originally built across from
the French Maginot Line, a similar stretch of bunkers and heavy
defenses intended to stop an enemy advance.

The German defenses included thousands of bunkers, tank
traps, obstacles, and other defenses that made a quick ground attack and breakthrough difficult, if not impossible. The line had
been reinforced and extended following the start of the war and
again after D-Day. It extended on German soil from the Netherlands south to Switzerland.

It did not, however, extend all the way to the North Sea. It might
be possible, therefore, to bypass it by attacking in the northern
Netherlands, crossing the Rhine, and driving down into Germany
from the north.

This was not as easy as it might sound. Much of the terrain had
been flooded, and there were several rivers in the area that could
be used as defense points, with a limited number of easily guarded
crossings.

Following their return to England, the 82nd, the 101st, and the
as-yet-untested 17th Airborne Divisions were joined with British airborne troops to form the First Airborne Allied Army. This
command had planned several actions, but none were carried out
because of the rapid change in ground conditions. Basically, our
armies were moving so fast that the plans became obsolete before
the jumps could be made.

Three divisions from the First Airborne Army—the 82nd, the
101st, and the British 1st Airborne Division, along with Polish
troops and some supporting units—would take the lead. Just un-

der 35,000 men would parachute or land by glider in the Netherlands, behind the lines of the German 84th Army Corps, seizing and holding key bridges that ran through the area. Highway 69, a key north-south route, would be taken by the troops, putting the major artery in Allied hands.

The airborne operation was the "Market" portion of the plan. It was to be followed by "Garden." A British Army corps would come north through the areas taken by the paratroopers, starting with the region west of Valkenwaard attacked by the 101st. By Day Two, they would arrive in the area secured by the 82nd, roughly around Grave and including a long bridge at Nijmegen. Two days later, they would arrive at the British positions in the far north, which included a major bridge at Arnhem. At that point, the attack would pivot over the crossings seized at Arnhem, breaking east through whatever German defenses had mustered there.

It was an ambitious plan. Aside from the success of the airborne attacks, it depended on the ground troops' ability to use Highway 69. While much of the area along the sides of the highway had been flooded or was too marshy to support vehicles, resistance along the highway route was expected to be light.

Things went well at first. Unlike most operations to this point in the war, a large portion of the airborne troops landed on target. My division, the 82nd, took most of their objectives—but failed to take the bridge at Nijmegen. Though they were able to control part of the bridgehead, the British were turned back at Arnhem, largely because the initial force aiming to take the city was too small. These two failures set the stage for what followed.

The Germans brought heavy reinforcements into the northern areas, cutting off British units. They secured Arnhem, cut off the British soldiers who had reached the bridgehead, and devastated attempts to resupply the division by air. By the end of the fourth day, the British survivors at the Arnhem bridgehead, out of ammunition and in many cases wounded, were captured.

In the meantime, the 82nd, joined by British ground forces, had taken Nijmegen. But it was too late. The Germans were able to block attempts to reach the British airborne troops farther north. In the south, troops taking Highway 69 were pummeled by artillery that had the road zeroed in. The British finally had to withdraw, crossing back over the southern bank of the Rhine after heavy losses. After withstanding a German counterattack, the 82nd hunkered down.

The 82nd was relieved on November 10. Some troops marched some twenty miles in the rain and an early snow before rendezvousing with trucks that were to remove them from the battle zone. They had spent a remarkable fifty days in combat, far longer than planned and an unusually long time for an airborne unit.

They were ready for a rest, and more. Their stay in the Low Countries had been costly, though after the fighting settled down the Dutch citizens proved as welcoming as the French had been. Now they were ready for some R&R in France.

It didn't last long.

A number of men were still on leave December 16, when news came that shocked Americans, not just those in uniform but nearly everyone back home. The Germans, thought to now to be on their deathbeds, had managed to launch a surprise attack in Belgium.

The American command was taken completely off guard.

While a secret system of intercepting and decrypting German communication nicknamed Ultra had provided excellent intelligence to this point in the war, somehow it and the entire intelligence community had missed the fact that three German armies with half a million men, over five hundred tanks, and another 650 self-propelled guns and tank destroyers had massed in the Ardennes Forest. Taking advantage of bad weather and attacking a front so quiet it was called "the Ghost Front," the Germans galloped through the American lines. By the night of December 18, their armies threatened the headquarters of the American Corps commander overseeing the area at Bastogne.

Desperate to stem the German advance, the Allies threw their best troops into the battle—including the 82nd and 101st.

There was a time when every schoolkid in America knew what happened next; I suspect a lot still do. The 101st arrived at Bastogne in the nick of time, fending off the Germans and refusing to surrender even when surrounded. Brigadier General Anthony McAuliffe, acting commander of the 101st, sent back a one-word reply to the Germans when told his force was surrounded and they must surrender:

"Nuts!"

The paratroopers held out until the day after Christmas, when a column of tanks and ground soldiers from Patton's army to the south broke through the defenses and relieved them.

The 101st was justly celebrated for their bravery in the harsh fight. But the 82nd deserves credit, too, for their efforts in the north.

Like the 101st, the 82nd arrived in trucks, driving through pouring rain and sleet. Where the 101st had assembled near Bastogne, the 82nd arrived at Werbomont. From there the troops moved forward to bridges that sat in the path of the Germans, blocked the Germans from capturing Trois Ponts, and fought a tough battle at Cheneux.

Stalled by tougher American resistance than they had hoped for, the Germans had already outrun their supply lines. They were far short of their objectives, Antwerp and Brussels. Most units hadn't even pushed beyond the Outhre River, west of Bastogne. Marche, a key city in the center of the bulge, remained in American hands. As the weather cleared, the fight shifted abruptly. With fresh troops arriving almost every hour and the cloud moving on so that fighter-bombers could join the fight, the Germans were doomed. Trying to regain momentum, they tried a counterattack in January, but failed. American armies on both sides of the salient began rolling them back.

Many men fought hard in the Bulge, not just the paratroopers. There had been about a quarter million American soldiers in the sector when the attack began; by the middle of January, there were over seven hundred thousand. The Germans were down to about two hundred tanks, many with barely enough fuel to get back to the German border. Our side had almost twenty-five hundred, with thousands more armored vehicles and guns. Twenty-two infantry divisions and eight armored divisions made up the core of the Allied force.

So a lot of guys participated. Not just the paratroopers. The Germans had gambled that they would catch the Allies off guard, and win either time to keep fighting, or even be able to sue for peace.

Instead, losing the gamble, they deprived themselves of weapons and men that might have been used on German soil.

The cost to us was not trivial. Between 75,000 and 90,000 American soldiers were killed, wounded, or captured during the Bulge battles. That's a sizable percentage of the 500,000 casualties we suffered from D-Day onward.

More than 23,000 of those casualties were men taken prisoner. The Germans began marching them back to Germany, sending some to camps as bad as mine. In other cases, they were simply marched and transported around; the Germans had no place to put them.

———————

Sometimes, they saved themselves the trouble.

On December 17, near the start of the offensive, eighty-four American soldiers who had surrendered were murdered by German SS troops, who began firing machine guns at them when they were assembled in a field. The incident became known as the Malmedy Massacre. It was later learned that the unit responsible for the murders was an SS troop, and word of it quickly spread through the troops.

Rumors about what happened at Malmedy circulated among troops at the front almost immediately. The incident sparked retaliation killings, especially of SS men. It is said that several commanders issued orders that prisoners would not be taken—in other words, kill anyone who tried to surrender.

But while it became infamous, the Malmedy Massacre was only one of many cases where soldiers trying to surrender were cut down, either a few at a time or en masse. It happened in Normandy, it happened at the Bulge; it must have happened everywhere in between and beyond.

———————

Until the Battle of the Bulge, the Allied command had considered the war all but won. A lot of the public back home did, too. The German onslaught, which was reported in detail by reporters who were in the area when it began, changed that. The confidence that they had felt evaporated. As the honor roll of the dead increased in the weekly newspaper listings, people realized that the war could go on for a lot longer, increasing the odds that their loved one would someday join the list.

ALIVE

Sometime in November—the exact date now seems impossible to determine, but our best guess is mid-month, before Thanksgiving—my parents received a brief notice saying that I was in fact alive, and that I was a prisoner of war.

How exactly the information got out—maybe through the International Red Cross and the German hospital—I have no idea. But the Army considered it reliable enough to take me off the MIA list and declare me alive.

I would guess it made them feel somewhat more hopeful.

What they would have thought had they known fully what that meant—what I was witnessing, what those around me were going through—I can't begin to say.

And truthfully, even I didn't know yet what the price of survival would be.

NINE

Opportunity

"GOOD LUCK"

Winter passed. The weather got warmer.

How long was that?

Months, unnumbered. Working it out now, this must have been March, or maybe very early April.

They must have had a quota at the coal mine, because they worked us hard every day; there were no days off.

Jim and I talked on the way to and from the mine.

Trying to escape—even if it meant getting shot—was better than a slow death. So we decided we'd try.

One night we came back from the mine. It had started to rain. For some reason, there were only four guards with us—two at the front, two at the rear.

We were somewhere in the middle.

There were bushes on the side of the road, about halfway back to the camp.

"Let's get out of here," whispered Tim.

We stepped out in the darkness.

"Good luck," hissed the guy behind me as we ran.

TEN

What Had to Be Done

HALT!

We knew there'd be a count as soon as the detail got back to the camp. That gave us ten, maybe twenty minutes.

We took off running down a little hill through the fields.

We saw a small town or village after we'd run for twenty minutes or so. By now it was starting to get light. Not full dawn, but just before.

As we got closer to the houses, someone saw us. He seemed to be a guard or policeman—probably a member of the Volkssturm. These home guards in the towns were usually older men who couldn't be drafted, in their fifties or sixties, or sometimes a soldier who'd lost an arm or was injured badly in the war. You could identify them by armbands, usually, though in some cases they had uniforms, often old or mismatched.

The man began yelling.

Halt!

Getting captured meant certain death. Jim and I spotted a barn near the outskirts and ran for it. He was fast behind us. Jim was a little ahead of me, and ran in looking for a weapon or maybe a place to hide. I stepped to the side of the doorway, flattening myself against the wall as the guy came in. He had drawn his pistol.

He started shooting.

A two-by-four was right by the door, probably used to lock it closed or prop it open. Not really thinking, I grabbed it and hit the German across the head.

Very, very hard.

All my energy, all my anger went into that blow. That two-by-four carried months of anger in it.

The policeman fell.

I hit him—how many times, I don't know, but it must have been enough to kill him.

Jim lay dead, a few yards away, shot in the head.

———

I took the German's gun, his holster, and two full magazines that he had in a pouch at his belt. I still have it today. It's a semi-automatic 9 mm pistol, made in Belgium. I'm not positive, but I think I believe it's an FN P35, which was manufactured during the war for the Nazis, though I've never had it checked out to be sure.

———

Jim was dead, and I was on my own. I ran out of the barn, worried that someone heard the gunshot and would sound the alarm.

I had no idea which direction to go in. I just ran until I came to a creek. By then I was hearing dogs barking; I thought they must be guards from the prison or the local police trying to track me.

I'd heard that dogs would lose your scent if you ran through water, so I jumped into the stream. It was wide—maybe twenty feet—but shallow, not more than a foot deep.

I walked in that stream for an hour or more, until the cold got to me. I must have gone three or four miles. With my legs starting to get numb, I climbed out into a field. I walked a ways and dropped down to rest in the cover.

That was the lowest point of my life. The cold, my soaked uniform, the fact that I was alone—there were many times when I came close to despair, but that moment, out of the creek, was the very worst.

Somehow I managed to get up. Maybe I had a flood of adrenaline—it wouldn't be the last time.

If there had been dogs or troops tracking me, they had lost my trail. But I was far from safe, and now so tired I could hardly walk, let alone run. I was pretty cold and in bad shape. My uniform was soaked to my thighs.

I finally spotted a small church and a cemetery not too far away. If I could get there, I thought, I might be able to bunk out for a while. It would be better than just collapsing in the open field.

When I got to the cemetery, it seemed to me a place where people wouldn't look. There were enough headstones to hide behind, and besides, I was too tired to go.

Thirst came over me. I saw a little vase of flowers with water on a fresh grave. I went down on my hands and knees, pulled out the flowers, and drank the water.

It tasted terrible, but it quenched my thirst. I crawled behind a headstone and lay down, to sleep or die.

I woke the next day, alive. No one had come for me. I was alive and free. Also hurting and hungry. I had no plan, and only the barest amount of hope.

I wanted to survive. That was all.

I stayed in the cemetery through the night and the next day. As I regained my senses, I realized that traveling at night would be far safer than during the day. I'd been taught how to follow the stars; I found the north star and figured out which way was west.

West was where our army was. How far away? It didn't matter. What I needed was direction, not distance. I would walk as far as I had to, until I either made it to safety or was killed. There was no other possibility.

I found a road westward and began following it. I had no idea where I was, but as long as I could see the sky I could reckon that I was going in the right direction.

On the third night, I saw a building forty or fifty feet off the road. It was a little house, with no lights. I thought I might pick up some food there.

What was my plan?

There was none.

What I was thinking—"thinking" might be too much of a word there—was this:

I'll barge in, take what I want. Leave.

I'd become a thief.

If I saw anyone, I would . . . scare them and grab what I wanted. Then run. Whatever had to be done.

I'd barge in, take food, escape.

It didn't work out that way.

I grabbed the door, pushed, barged in—and saw a Volkssturm

militiaman not five feet from me. He was an older man, and surprised—stunned—to see me.

I shot him dead, found some food near him in the room—hard bread—then took off.

I must have run eight or ten miles after that. Finally, exhausted, I found a patch of trees and brush and went there to hide.

The next night, or maybe a night or two later, I saw a barn a few feet from the road. Thinking I might find some potatoes or other food inside, I walked to it carefully. By now it was very late, and positive it would be empty, I went in through the door—only to find two members of the Volkssturm a few feet away, chatting.

I'd stumbled into a small command post or meeting place of some sort.

The men looked over, startled. One was sixty, maybe. The other just a teen.

I fired point blank into each of them, quick succession, boom, boom, boom, then ran.

No food, no nothing. Just more fear.

I killed the men, I'm sure. At that range, in that small a space, there's no way the bullets could miss. Even if the men didn't die right away, they would have bled to death before help got there.

They were easy targets, easy victims. Not soldiers, really, despite insignia. Poor villagers pressed into service, doing a job they probably didn't even care for.

I didn't think about that then. I wasn't thinking at all, just doing. I'd scraped down below a thinking person, to an animal, to something worse.

I hated Germans. All of them. SS guards, grenadiers,

Volkssturm, farmers, teenagers. Every man, woman, and child. I had a terrible, terrible hate of each and every one.

From the distance now of so many years, there are reasons and excuses—I'd been beaten and starved and tortured. I'd seen the very worst humans could do. I was sleep and food deprived. I was desperate to survive.

I knew if I was caught—when I was caught—I was dead.

Maybe with work it can be made to sound pretty on the page, or almost pretty. But it was none of that. It was what had to be done. With hatred in my heart.

Savagery.

———————

I slept in the woods the rest of that night and into the day. When it was dark, I started out again.

You know, when you leave three people behind you, shot dead or even just wounded, people realize there's someone on the loose. I was leaving a trail—not too smart.

I had to keep moving.

And find some food.

———————

Another night, more running—I'm not sure when exactly this was, whether it was just a day later or two or three or more. I found another building, far from everything else. It looked like a cottage or maybe a guard post.

This time I was deliberate. I saw there was a German inside, a man in uniform. This man I was going to kill. He was a soldier in uniform, a man I'd enlisted to kill, a warrior worthy of death.

I barged in again. So far behind the lines, no one took precautions, no one was on their guard as they should have been.

He wasn't far away from me when I shot him.

This time, I checked and made sure he was dead before looking for food. He had a knapsack; inside was some sausage, cheese, and very hard, stale bread. My dinner.

I don't know if he'd just gotten there or was about to start a patrol or what. I've often thought about it without coming to any conclusions. I didn't know at the time that the war was coming very close. Some soldiers were running away; maybe he was one. Or maybe he was part of a force looking for me. All I knew was that I was hungry, and he'd given me dinner.

I made another eight or ten miles that night before I found a good wooded area. I went into the trees and hid in a spot where I could see the road.

A little later, I heard artillery—our artillery, I thought. That gave me a lot of hope. If I could just make it a little while longer, I was bound to find our guys and be rescued.

If I could just survive.

SHAME

I went on like that, preying on German soldiers or Volkssturm late at night on the road. The soldiers always carried knapsacks with food, and there'd always be water. These men weren't terribly alert; they thought they were safe. Or they were like me when I first jumped into Normandy, naïve about what war really means.

There'd be a guy walking on the road, going from one point

to another. I'd just walk right up; maybe he saw me and thought I was a villager. Maybe he didn't see me because I snuck up, or my clothes, blacked from the mine, made me almost invisible.

Pistol, close range.

I was a guerrilla, waging war behind the lines as I'd been trained. A paratrooper on the lam. Or a desperate man, doing what he had to do to survive.

Most nights, I found no one. I didn't take the crazy risks I had before. Now I just watched for a single man on the road, too far from town to be heard, but close enough to think he was safe.

How many, I'm not sure. Maybe four times, or three. Less than a handful.

I've never spoken of these things before, not even to my family. I've been ashamed of them. I'm ashamed of them still.

Sometimes when I'm not doing anything, I think about these things. They still bother me.

I wasn't a hero. I was a savage. Worse. A killer and a thief. I did what had to be done to survive.

Few people know how terrible that is, how deep your desperation becomes. Few people understand how strong hatred can be, and how the two feed on each other.

And how long it can last. Even today, if the guards who beat me in the mine were to suddenly appear before me, I would kill them and feel no remorse.

Even though we're old men, far from the war, well beyond those days, I'd kill each one with any means I had.

YANKEE! YANKEE!

———————————

I spent about two weeks like that, running at night, trying to stay going west. A few times I stole food, but mostly I was hungry and walked. Eight, ten miles at night.

I was an animal, desperate, willing to do the most vile things imaginable if it meant surviving.

Or, I was a one-man wrecking crew behind enemy lines, killing the enemy as I'd been trained to do.

It depends on how you see it, how you tell it, how it's heard. In most books on the war, it would be the latter, the tale of a marauder against the odds. Which would be true enough.

But I see it, often now, as the first, and feel ashamed. People assure me it was the second, say I was heroic, brave, courageous. I nod, but my feelings don't totally change.

Was there a line I wouldn't cross? Something I wouldn't do to survive?

I don't know. I suppose there must have been.

But . . .

———————————

One morning a little before dawn, I was near a house at the edge of a hamlet where I saw a well. Thirsty, I figured I'd take a chance getting water, even though the well was a little close to the building and it was getting light.

Stupid.

I had just started pumping the well, when out comes a young woman, maybe seventeen, walking with a bucket right to me. She saw me before I saw her, dropped her bucket, and wheeled to run.

"Yankee! Yankee! Yankee!" she screamed.

An instant to decide:

Do I live or die?

I had to survive. I raised my gun and shot her.

———————————

If you don't think that haunts you, even seventy-five years after the fact, you don't know the human soul.

It's a terrible thing to know how deep the need to survive is, and what it can push you to do.

ELEVEN

Home

PATTON'S ARMY

By the end of January, the Western Allies had regained the ground they'd lost in the Bulge. Poised on the frontier of Germany, they regrouped for a new push to Berlin. The Soviet Red Army, meanwhile, had arrived in Warsaw and crossed into East Prussia on the eastern border of Germany. Hitler, holed up in a Berlin bunker, gave orders forbidding retreat without his approval, but units retreated anyway.

Already deep on German soil, General Courtney Hodges's First Army crossed the Rhine in early March during the Battle of Remagen, a city on the western bank of the river. German combat engineers failed to blow the Ludendorff Bridge; our guys seized it.

Holding the bridge gave our troops a way to penetrate the last natural boundary between them and Germany's heartland. Realizing how important the crossing was, the German army spent the next several days trying to destroy it. Their attacks ranged from armored assaults to mortar salvos, floating mines, and, according to some, the first tactical bombing mission of a jet-engined bomber, Germany's Arado Ar 234B-2. All failed. First Army expanded the bridgehead, opening the way for a flood of troops.

Operating to First Army's south, General Patton's Third Army reached the Rhine on March 21; Patton had six battalions across before the sun rose March 23. A bridge was thrown up by combat engineers, and the Americans now had a second major crossing, one that led to southern Germany, Austria, and the Czech Republic.

The rapid advances by the Allies had not spared the civilian populations, even though they weren't directly targeted. Farms, villages, cities suffered as the armies wrestled.

The destruction was remarkable. It even moved Patton, not known for his compassion toward the enemy, to pity. In a letter to his wife March 23, he told her:

The displaced person is a problem. They are streaming back utterly forlorn. I saw one woman with a perambulator full of her worldly goods sitting by it on a hill crying. An old man with a wheelbarrow and three little children wringing his hands. A woman with five children and a tin cup crying. In hundreds of villages there is not a living thing, not even a chicken. Most of the houses are heaps of stones. They brought it on themselves, but these poor peasants are not responsible.

And then, as often with Patton, he had another thought:

I am getting soft? I did most of it.

It was the terrible ambiguity of the war, of all wars—to do what had to be done, many who weren't "guilty" had to suffer.

Like Hodges's First Army, Patton's Third consisted of different corps, each composed of infantry and armored divisions and smaller, specialized units. By late spring 1945, well over half a million men and eighteen divisions were in the Third Army, advancing across the southern portion of Germany.

During the first week of April, an armored strike force from the 4th Division had attempted to capture Field Marshal Albert Kesselring. Driving deep into Germany, they missed the key Nazi commander. Instead, they discovered a Nazi extermination or death camp in Ohrdruf. There were more than 3,200 naked bodies in shallow graves. Ohrdruf was a satellite of Buchenwald, a massive German concentration complex whose satellites or subcamps were used to hold, exterminate, and work to death over a quarter million people, from Jews to political prisoners to prisoners of war.

It was the first concentration camp liberated by American forces. It would not be the last.

THE RETREAT

I was somewhere to the east of the Third Army's advance, though I had no idea that they were headed in my direction. Each night I moved westward as far as I dared, and as far as my legs and fear would take me. My ambushes so far didn't make me more confident; they had almost the opposite effect, as if I thought I had only a certain amount of luck, and feared I'd used it all.

I wasn't as hungry as I'd been as the days went on. Or maybe

I was, but had learned to put the feeling aside. I felt so much else that a hunger pang barely registered.

I can't even tell you what else I did those days, pushing through southern Germany. Mostly I avoided people.

———————

I'd holed up in a wooded copse to hide in one night when I heard artillery again. This was loud, and I knew from the sound it was ours. It got louder and louder, and at dawn I heard noises I hadn't heard before—people traveling along the road.

Civilians. Fleeing with everything they had.

I was about a hundred yards away, maybe a little more, from the road—close enough to see what was happening without being seen. I looked out from the brush and saw people streaming down the road, some with horse-drawn wagons and carts. They were moving fast.

Two hours later, I saw infantry moving down the road.

German soldiers. A lot of them. Hundreds, on foot and in trucks.

Then tanks and mobile guns. Eighty-eights. It was a long column of troops, obviously beating a hasty retreat.

I was so amazed at what I was seeing that I didn't even think to hide myself. I suppose anyone seeing me from that distance would think I was just a civilian. I stood and stared, barely comprehending as a buzz in the distance grew. The sound was an airplane, a small one—I looked above and spotted a little Piper Cub spotter plane circling.

Cleary, he was looking for these guys.

The Germans were smart. They didn't fire at the little plane, knowing it would tell the spotter where they were.

But it didn't matter. Ten minutes later, maybe fifteen, artillery shells began falling on the road. The column was still passing through. A shell hit a tank, wrecking it and forcing the column to stop.

Shells kept falling on the road as I cowered. I was far enough from the road—and whoever was firing the artillery had good enough coordinates and fire discipline—that I wasn't hit. But plenty of Germans were. I heard cries of pain, desperate pleas.

The Germans who weren't killed managed to keep going, escaping with their wounded.

I felt no sorrow for them, no compassion. But I didn't feel any joy, either. I felt nothing. I'd grown to understand war and survival completely.

The fires burned into the night. I stayed where I was.

I woke the next morning to the sound of tanks coming down the road. I got up, thinking at first that they were more German tanks. But the shapes were wrong.

Our tanks. American tanks.

I was too scared to move. It wouldn't have made sense—these guys would have shot at anything in the road or nearby, I'm sure. I stayed where I was, hunkered down as they pursued the Germans. I'm sure they knew they weren't far ahead.

The Americans quickly pushed and towed the wrecked German vehicles off the road. Trucks followed with infantrymen.

A few hours passed. I stayed where I was. I didn't want some trigger-happy guy to shoot me because I didn't know the password. After you've been in combat a while, you don't think twice about shooting.

Things died down, and I started making my way toward the road, a few yards at a time, not sure yet how to make contact.

Finally, a Jeep with a single radioman came up the road. He stopped to take a look and maybe make a radio call.

That was my chance. If he was occupied with the radio, he'd be less likely to shoot me. Especially with the rifle in the Jeep out of reach, or at least out of my sight.

I snuck out of the brush, walking as quietly as I could, and tapped him on the shoulder.

He just about jumped to the clouds.

"What are you doing? Where are you going?" the radioman demanded.

He took a breath, calming down, realizing I guess that I wasn't out to kill him. Then his eyes just about crossed.

"You look like a ragman," he said.

"I'm an American," I told him. "I escaped from a prison camp. I'm an American. Help me."

MEMORY

Thinking back on this now, it all seems incredible. The two weeks of being a savage, the column of Germans, the attack.

Did it all happen exactly as I remember?

I believe so. Some of it, I think, was worse.

A few of the details now are jumbled in my memory. I was further or closer to this and that. I saw bits and pieces of things, and my mind supplied the rest. Details have slipped away—or maybe hid themselves from the part of the brain that can't take such horror.

I know I was very lucky. So many times I could have been killed, and not just by the Germans. A stray bomb, a shell, the man in the Jeep. I could have slipped in the stream, hit my head, and drowned unconscious. If I'd been in a more important place with bigger towns, or if the soldiers stationed there had been more competent or better trained, I'd have met my match within a day or two. Had I been captured a year earlier and then escaped, the Germans would have put a lot more effort into capturing me. With the Allies pressing in from all sides, I wasn't really worth the effort.

The radioman put me in his Jeep and took me back to his headquarters.

I can't tell you which unit it was. It must have been about four miles back from where I'd been picked up.

The captain there looked at me and said, "You look like a sorry mess."

I had to agree. I told him what had happened. I'd gone maybe a hundred miles and spent two weeks ravaging the countryside.

Guesses.

I don't remember any questions about whether I was an American or not, let alone suspicions that I might be a spy. No one even asked to see my dog tags. It was probably pretty obvious I was an American from the way I spoke, and my guess is that at that point in the war, our guys weren't too worried about spies.

Intel on the enemy was a different matter. The captain asked me a few questions about what I'd seen. It must have been obvious that I had no information that could help them, because our conversation didn't last all that long. He gave me a new uniform and let me clean up a bit.

The unit had picked up some other escapees and sent them back to France; he said he'd send me there, too. There was an airstrip not all that far away; another Jeep ride, and I was looking at a C-47 being packed with the wounded. They took me along, and a few hours and another plane ride or two later, I was in France.

Free France.

LUCKY STRIKE

I was taken to a camp called Lucky Strike.

Lucky Strike was the name of a very popular brand of cigarettes, before, during, and after the war. In this case, its name had been appropriated by a large base originally set up to help process soldiers as they were being brought into Europe. It was one of several "cigarette camps" with similar missions, so named because most were given the names of popular brands of cigarettes. There was Pall Mall, Philip Morris, Old Gold, and a few others.

The camps were near Marseilles in the south, and Le Havre in the north; both cities were major ports that were used to ship troops into the fight. Lucky Strike was in Normandy near Saint-Valery at San Riquie en Caux.

Things had changed a lot in northwestern France since I'd been there eight or nine months before. Then this place had been a German airfield, probably a prime target for bombers in the buildup to the landings. Now it was a mass of canvas tents—American tents, American soldiers, American doctors, and even nurses. The camp's purpose was evolving from an entrance to Europe to an exit; it had begun processing POWs liberated from the western portion of Germany in March. It would eventually handle thousands of men a week as they shipped home, but when I arrived it was relatively quiet.

The first thing the docs at the camp did when I arrived was delouse me. My clothes were burned, and I was showered with DDT, the Army's standard delousing chemical during the war. I took a *real* shower—boy did that water feel good. I stayed under so long I'm sure I was waterlogged. Then I got dressed in the new uniform they gave me, and went for something to eat.

Solid food and a lot of it was what I wanted. I wasn't just hungry; I was famished. I weighed 90 pounds when I arrived. Compare that to the 150 when I left for England.

The doctors and nurses were very nice. They were also very smart. Rather than telling me that I had to build my weight up slowly, they let me eat anything I wanted that first day.

Anything?

I ate it all: hamburgers, milk shakes, whatever. They kept the food coming.

Sure enough, I got really sick, really fast.

From there on, I was ready to listen to their advice.

They were extremely kind, the nurses especially. I went exploring. Lucky Strike was more like a city than an army camp. You could get lost in it—but it had to be big, as it had housed close to sixty thousand at its peak. There was a bar, a movie theater, and of course a fully equipped field hospital. I didn't have it to myself, and I wouldn't say the place was empty, but there weren't nearly so many men that it felt crowded.

I drank a lot of milk shakes—slowly—and quickly added weight. Good food—rich soups, thick steaks. The first steaks I had in Europe. Aside from being exhausted and well underweight, I was in what the doctors declared was surprisingly decent shape despite my time in the mines and prison camp. The Germans who had operated on me in Paris had done a very good job removing the shrapnel. I still had pieces near my spine. While those could only be removed in a better-equipped facility, I was in no immediate danger from them. The Army would take care of that after I gained a little more strength.

I didn't write home. I figured I'd be home before the mail got there.

And what would I have said anyway?

They kept me at the camp maybe three weeks, waiting for me to get a little more fat on my bones. They interrogated me on what I'd been through. I told them everything I could remember; I doubt now it was of much use to them, but I certainly hoped it would be at the time.

Finally, I was issued new orders—report to a hospital in Texas and prepare to give up the metal the Germans had put in my back. In the meantime, I was to enjoy a sixty-day furlough, as well as an all-expenses-paid trip back to the States via airplane.

I found my plane and happily headed home. For some reason I didn't stop to call or telegraph my parents or Arlene that I was on my way. I just went.

HOME

My plane landed in New York. I checked in at camp, then soon was on my way by train to Chicago and finally the local to Clinton.

I got off in the middle of the day. Clinton had changed in the two years or so since I'd been gone, but not so much that I couldn't find my way home. I found a bus and headed to the house.

My youngest sister was playing outside when I got off and walked across the railroad tracks. She saw me and ran into the house to tell my mom.

"I think Heinie's home."

The family hadn't received any word that I had escaped, let alone that I had reached our lines, been rescued, spent time in the hospital, or was coming home. The war in Europe was still raging. As far as they knew, I was dead. Or maybe in a prison camp somewhere.

I stopped in the yard, taking it in. I'd seen the house so many times in my mind. It looked exactly the same.

I walked to the door, opened it.

There was no rush of excitement, no big hugs or kisses. My mother said hello. That was it. My dad just shrugged. "You're back."

It was as if I'd just gone down to the store to grab a bottle of milk and come back.

Yet it didn't seem odd to me at all. That was the way my family was. There were no big signs of emotion. Or anything else—I'd get all of that and more from Arlene.

Kisses and hugs and more—nothing X-rated, but so much love when I found her at home a few hours later that I felt a thrill beyond anything, beyond falling from planes, beyond even surviving.

TWELVE

Survival's Rewards

VE DAY AND BEYOND

Tuesday, May 8, 1945.

I'd only been home for a few weeks, still enjoying my furlough and recovering. I was still gaining weight, spending as much time as I could with Arlene, and just happy to be alive and free.

The news came: Germany had surrendered.

The war in Europe was over.

Germany had been occupied.

Hitler was dead.

We'd won.

It wasn't the exact end of the war, of course. We knew there was more fighting ahead. Friends were still deployed, including Arlene's brothers. I'd known it was coming soon—it was obvious when I was on the run, probably the reason I was able to make it so far, most likely the reason I was alive. The Germans had far more things to worry about as their defenses and country collapsed than an escaped prisoner roving their countryside.

Still, it was an end. A good one.

We celebrated it. Yeah. I think everybody had a headache the next day. Even I did.

The celebration in Clinton wasn't as crazy as what you see in the old photos and newsreels—I don't think there were any sailors kissing girls on the street. But the church bells rang, and we could all feel that huge load fall off our shoulders. I can still remember the feeling of driving in a car, hanging out the window, feeling the breeze against my face.

Freedom whispering in my ear as I shouted hello and hurray.

Arlene and I visited our grandmothers. Family and ties to the past, our past—it all suddenly seemed important.

This is terrible to say, but looking back I think I felt as if we should have gotten a little more out of that war. I'd seen all the terrible things the Nazis had done. How do you make up for that?

We ended up helping them rebuild, rather than really punishing them.

That was right, I guess. Being magnanimous. But deep inside, a little part of me felt—I guess ungenerous. I guess like there should have been some way that they made up for it.

But mostly I felt relief. Mostly I felt like I wanted to get on with my life. With Arlene, in Clinton, in America.

We went to a local jeweler and picked out an engagement ring. A nice diamond, nicer than the one I'd "lost" in England.

Arlene has a funny story about that. Not long after I got home, I think we were at the movies, I told her, I want to show you something. It's been with me the whole time.

She thought I was going to show her the ring I'd bought in England. What I showed her was her photo, which had been with me all the time, that and the Bible.

I guess she was disappointed, but to me, that photo was worth a thousand diamonds. It connected me to her better than my memory could. Maybe it was one of the reasons I was able to survive.

I got my own surprise when I went down to city hall for the marriage license—because I wasn't yet twenty-one, the clerk said I wasn't old enough to get married without my parents' permission. I had to go back to the house and get my mother to vouch for me.

Old enough to fight in a war; not old enough to get married. Something there doesn't add up.

———————

Arlene's explanations about how she had prayed for me to come home convinced me that, while I had been very lucky, maybe her prayers had something to do with that luck. Her faith in God was deep. I thought about the two friends I'd seen die with a peace on their faces, and that question I had asked myself so many months before:

Would I be able to die so peacefully?

Maybe I would, if I had faith. I started taking lessons with Arlene's Lutheran pastor. He baptized and confirmed me. I became a Lutheran and a firm believer in God. As time has gone on, my wife and I have found that our faith is not defined by a specific denomination, but remains as strong as ever.

Arlene and I got married July 1. It was a small wedding. The ceremony was at the parson's house at the Zion Lutheran Church, where Arlene was a parishioner. After the ceremony, we went to her parents' house to celebrate with our families and a few friends.

I don't know how her mom and dad pulled it off, and Arlene doesn't, either. Her mother had asked Arlene's aunts to help by bringing in some of their favorite dishes, and somehow they turned that small little house into a palace full of laughter and plenty to eat and drink. Our wedding cake was a sponge cake—just getting the sugar they needed was tough, because of rationing; sugar was in very short supply. But the ladies put their resources together, and their heads, and pulled it off.

Her dad's job that day was serving beer in the garage—simple but vital.

Our honeymoon was in town—we celebrated in the front rooms of the house her grandmother had turned into a boarding-house. An aunt was living there, and she gave up the place for a few days so we could be alone.

It was a good thing, as I didn't have a house of my own. In fact, I didn't even have pajamas, not with me, anyway. I'd been so excited to get on with the ceremony and all that I hadn't brought anything but the clothes on my back to the parson's home. I had to enlist two of her aunts for a ride to my parents' house, where I retrieved my things and then went to enjoy my first night as a married man.

The next order of business was getting rid of the shrapnel that the German doctors in Paris had left in my back. The Army sent me down to Texas for the operation. It went well—though even those doctors decided that it was best to leave a few small scraps in there rather than risk damage to my spine. I guess there's no harm, as I seem to have gotten along all these years without much trouble or setting off too many metal detectors.

In August, the United States dropped two atomic bombs on Japan, and the war ended. There were more celebrations. Each time one of Arlene's brothers or a friend came home, there was another. Until finally, we were all back.

At the end of 1945, after I'd healed a bit from my surgery, the Army decided they'd had enough of me. I was given an honorable discharge. I had been recently promoted to corporal, and the clerks would record that I was worthy of two Bronze Stars, a Purple Heart, and a Good Conduct Medal. My unit, meanwhile, had received a Distinguished Unit Citation with Oak Cluster—in other words, two such awards for bravery and accomplishment in battle. There were a lot of heroes.

Not me. But I was lucky enough to serve with them.

Arlene's father gave us a lot next to their house in town, and she and I went to work building our first house. I dug the foundation with the help of some horses, painstakingly scooping out the dirt for a basement. We built it together, stick by stick.

It still stands.

Eventually we built another, and later another, where we still live. Not large, but comfortable enough to raise a family. With Arlene's help, I built a construction company. We made a variety of buildings, but I guess I'm most proud of the work we did for the schools. America was growing, and education was a big need. I made it a rule to do good work, to get it done on time and on budget. A lot of times that meant working after dinner, but hard work was nothing to shy away from. Arlene helped by doing the books, but like a lot of women, most of her time was spent on the kids and the house. She was a tremendous worker. Side by side, we built a family and a business, helping the community we were part of.

====================

THIRTEEN

Going Back

For fifty years, I didn't talk about the war.

There were a few reasons. One was that I was simply busy getting on with things. That was the case for most people. Guys came back, renewed relationships, or started new ones. They went to work, got married, got busy with their lives. I had a business that became pretty large, and that took up a lot of time.

And I didn't want to touch my memories.

I kept them away. Some men probed the past—checking with old units, uncovering things they didn't know at the time. I didn't want to do any of that. I didn't want to know the specifics of where I had been, where the prison camp was, not even the unit I was attached to. I didn't want to make connections with the people I'd served with, even vague connections.

I stayed away, physically as well as mentally. Let it all be forgotten. So much of it was.

There were times right after the war when I needed to be alone. I'd be in a bad mood and go off by myself.

I knew the things I did, and what I'd seen. I knew what it feels like to see a friend die. To see people with their limbs off. Bodies stacked by a barbed wire fence.

I knew what it feels like to be hit with a rifle butt. To be worked over.

I knew hatred, and murderous intent.

I knew how low a man has to go to survive.

It's something I really didn't want to remember.

Over the years, people at the Department of Veterans Affairs, the VA, asked me if I had bad memories. I said yes, but I didn't want to go over them.

"Well then, you must be well enough to take care of it yourself," they'd say. And I guess they were right. I never gave details when my family asked. I'd just say, "I did what I had to do."

What I had to do to survive. Your job as a soldier is to kill people. It's not something you ought to brag about.

Escaping, I'd done what had to be done. I knew I *had* to do it, but that didn't make it any easier deep down to feel comfortable with it.

The truth was, the biggest reason I didn't talk much was that I was ashamed of what I had to do to survive. Of killing. I couldn't be proud of what I'd had to do behind the lines, even if I had trained for it, even if it was the stuff of movies.

I just couldn't be proud of it. The opposite—ashamed.

And if that's how I felt, how would someone who wasn't there, who didn't know the dark reality—how would they even believe these things were possible? That all men and women are capable of that, if they want to survive?

How many people really believe that now?

They don't want to believe the things people do to other people. They even downplay the Holocaust. I know it happened. I saw it. I know they did.

Sometimes people ask me what it was like to have to kill men in war.

I don't tell them. They don't really want to know, I think—or they would be shocked. You don't feel anything, not after a while. Later is different, but at that moment, nothing. Relief for an instant that you're not the one dead, then move on.

I tell them, "war is war." Most people let it go and don't really push it.

How many people did you kill?

I've been asked that when I've spoken.

I just say, "war is war."

We had a lot of close combat. Guy comes over a hedgerow at you, or you go over, you see someone, and you shoot him.

That's combat. That's war. Do what needs to be done, and move on.

———————————

I'd been an atheist, more or less, through the war. Even with a Bible in my pocket, I can't say that I really understood God or found religion.

Arlene brought me to it. Her faith in me coming back, her trust in God—that was a powerful thing. I started going to church. I kept reading the Bible. I guess I learned to pray, and to trust, the way she had.

I also remembered again my two buddies who'd died on the battlefield with peace in their hearts and on their faces. Their faith was another example for me.

But as powerful as all of that became, I didn't feel it related to what I'd been through, and it didn't push me to talk about the war in any way.

Our family believed in serving the country. My eldest son, Dennis, served in Vietnam, with two deployments there. Two of my grandsons, Phillip and Aaron, joined the 82nd Airborne. So did a great-grandson, Nathaniel.

My grandsons started asking a lot of questions. Little by little, I opened up.

Others found out. I was asked to speak, and reluctantly agreed. Young people need to know about the war, and about their past. So I started to share.

I don't tell the entire story. Not even here. Some of it is too grim. And some of it—words really can't convey exactly what happened. There are some feelings that are beyond expression. Without taking you physically back to Normandy, or that hospital in Paris, or God forbid the mines, I can't give you the exact and full picture.

The terror.

The fear.

The knowledge of what we are capable of doing when it must be done.

Or the horror when you realize how dark evil truly can be, and that men are capable of it.

———————

The youngest generation doesn't know that much about the war. I tell them. I don't know if it'll matter to anyone in ten years.

We're obsolete already. Most of us are gone. I was one of the younger ones.

I went to France and visited Normandy in 1986 with my wife and some of my family. I didn't want to go. But Arlene, my son, and his wife insisted, and when I got there, I felt better. Having them along changed things.

We found the location of a foxhole I'd been in near the du-Pont bridgehead. We saw the road where I'd blown up that tank, and killed my first enemy soldier close-up.

We sat on a bench near the water and had some Calvados while I told them what had happened some fifty years before. The river that day was so narrow—on D-Day the area looked more like a lake than a farm—they had a hard time at first imagining it.

The spot where the tank had been that night was just a quiet little intersection now, out in hedgerow country. Just another road in the bocage.

We also found the house I'd fallen into in Sainte-Mère-Église.

The door I'd gone out and the wall I'd jumped, or a rebuilt facsimile, were still there. I hadn't gotten much of a look at the garden that night, but I don't think it was all that different.

I wasn't about to run that route again; one of my sons did, a few years later, and told me it would have taken not much more than a minute or two to get from the wall to the area outside the center of town.

"Longer, if someone is shooting at you," he said.

No, I thought. You would run a lot faster. It would only seem a lot longer.

We spent several days in Sainte-Mère-Église, using it as a base to explore the area. It's quite a tourist hub these days. While there have been many changes, a surprising amount has been restored more or less the way it was. There are plenty of monuments and plaques, a recent museum, and even a dummy paratrooper hanging from the church steeple. I had little trouble getting my bearings.

Arlene says I had a few tears in my eyes as we wandered around.

Later, we visited the cemetery—remains had not yet been moved over to the big cemetery near the beaches. We looked up the crosses of men I knew.

More tears there, I'm sure.

I didn't talk to many people. I didn't want to get into long conversations about the war; I just wanted to see the place again with my family. I hadn't wanted to come, but by the end of the trip, I was sorry I hadn't planned to stay longer.

The French have not forgotten the war, nor those who sacrificed to give them back their freedom. Even so, life goes on. Take away the monuments and museum and all the rest, and you might never imagine the place knew war; it's just a nice, peaceful, quiet little village a few miles from a very beautiful beach and ocean.

We were in a restaurant one night, and someone at a nearby table overheard our conversation. They bought us a bottle of wine as a way of saying thank you for having helped their country all those many years ago.

It was a kind and sweet gesture. The French are like that. Their president himself honored me with the French Legion of Honor at a ceremony in Washington in 2007. They made quite a fuss. It was really too much.

"You are a hero to France," said the president.

"The French have been so good to me," I answered.

The award and a photo are on the wall of my office in the basement, along with some other memories and mementos.

I kept the gun I took from the Volkssturm trooper there. My medals are nearby. There are some models on a shelf, including one of a C-47.

And the Bible I carried, and Arlene's photo, are there as well.

I'm an old fellow now, ninety-five. There may be parts of this I've misremembered, and many other parts I know for sure I've forgotten. Names, certainly. Reading it over, it seems barely believable.

Except for what I felt. The fear. The shame. The joy at having survived. Those are hard in my chest, firm in my brain.

Only a few of the men who jumped into Normandy are remembered by name today. That's doubly true for the hundreds of thousands who fought. Each one of us had a background and a family, a community we came from, parents, maybe someone who knew, just knew, we'd be back. Time has faded much of our stories, robbed the few of us still living of many details. But what does remain is the notion that some things are worth sacrificing for, and that survival has a purpose. Surviving can be a terrible ordeal; it can take us into the dark places of the human soul; it can make us question what we believe, and even make us ashamed of what we must do.

It has its price, but it has its rewards as well. Those of us who survived the war, doing whatever had to be done, knew both. I pray that you, too, may know the rewards, and never have to pay the price yourself.

God forgive me for what I had to do to survive. God forgive us all.

Collaborator's Note

I first met Henry on D-Day 2019, seventy-five years after he had jumped into Normandy. We'd come to Rock Island, the home of First Army, to talk about what had happened that day. Henry was the star. Everyone in the room and those connected via video around the world listened breathlessly as he described in simple words what it had been like to parachute into Normandy in the early morning of June 6, 1944. His understated account of the German defenses and counterattacks on D-Day itself brought the battle to life.

But there was a lot more to his story. A few weeks after D-Day, well before the American breakthrough that would make the end of the war inevitable, Henry told us, he had been captured in a hedgerow battle. He'd been taken to a POW camp and put to work in a horrific coal mine. He'd managed to escape, spending two weeks on the run behind enemy lines, doing things that still haunted him.

The officers and enlisted in the room, most of whom were already familiar with the story and had been to war themselves, listened in awe. Even the general.

Henry's tale made clear what that war was really like. Too often, books based on personal experiences glance over the painful decisions and brutal ethos of survival. The triumph is there, but the ambiguity of actions that under other circumstances would be considered murder is glossed over. When these are addressed in third-person histories, it is very difficult to conjure the immediacy and emotional impact of a memoir.

But telling such tales is difficult. As Henry relates here, the events still haunt him terribly. He did what had to be done to survive, as he often says, yet that simple fact contains within it vast complications. Human beings are capable of great things. But they are also capable of great evil, as Henry saw at the edge of the death camp and beyond. We feel innately that there is a sharp line between the things that must be done to survive and those that are clearly evil, yet people of conscience are so repulsed by acts of evil that inevitably they question any parallel, no matter how faint. Knowing how strong the biological impulse to survive is means knowing that there are dark possibilities in the human heart; experiencing the needs of the former inevitably suggests the power of the latter.

Then comes the question—where do I draw the line? Survival is a biological imperative, baked into our genes. But it can also be an excuse: I need to survive, therefore it is right to lie, proper to steal, justifiable to kill, as long as I live.

Henry's ordeal behind enemy lines could easily have broken him, but he was made of stronger stuff. He not only managed to survive, but on his return to America he reached great heights in his community, building schools and homes. These achievements did not erase the memory of his struggle; rather, they made it more poignant. In the end, he remained ashamed not just of what he had done to survive as an escapee, but of his need to kill his enemy on the battlefield. It was not that he thought he wasn't justified; he understood intellectually that war demands things a soldier must fulfill. He knew that individually each action flowed from a simple choice: kill or be killed. But the necessity to make those choices was terrible in itself; to do what had to be done required a hard and uncomforting view of himself, and humankind.

For those reasons, he hadn't talked about the war in any sort of depth for some fifty years. Even when he started speaking of it in the late 1990s, he generally skimmed over what he had to do as an escapee.

Yet that was surely the most poignant part of his story—the part that could instruct all of us, far more than the information about how heavy the pack of explosives he carried on D-Day was, or how loud the mortar shells were when they exploded.

I can't say that I talked him into sharing that part of his story. He made that decision on his own, compelled I think by the same unconscious drive that guided him following the war. He felt a need to tell people what war really is, even if he winced as he spoke the words.

The details came haltingly, over a long period. There is more to the story, as he freely admitted here and to me several times—things too awful, at least in his mind, to share. There are limits to communication, but not to fear. Recounting the past inevitably conjures some of its emotion back. The sustained terror that accompanied his survival can only be handled in small bits, even now.

World War II has sometimes been called the "Good War."

That's bull. There are no good wars. There are *necessary* wars, and justifiable wars; that war was both. There are wars that must be fought to continue and even steer civilization's evolution toward a higher plane; World War II certainly qualifies. There are wars that must be won in order for us as human beings to survive; no one could argue that World War II was not that as well.

But it was not "good." It was ugly, as all wars are. Civilians were directly targeted again and again as a necessary part of waging the battle. The lines between combatant and noncombatant were far less clear in many circumstances than many history books would have us believe. Collateral damage was far greater than is generally spoken of. The emotional consequences of the war— post-traumatic stress disorder among them—were as prevalent among the fighters then as they have been in our recent conflicts.

Henry has no need for penance; he did what had to be done. But I don't think it's a coincidence that after the war he devoted himself to building things. Creating schools where students could learn wasn't a payback; he fulfilled no debt when he built a house to shelter a family. It was all a business, and a good one.

Yet at the same time, it was a contribution to the health and strength of his community, and by extension to America at large. It was the good side of human nature, the side of nurturing and progress. It was, in short, the reason the need to survive is so strong.

Ultimately, survival is not a shadow of evil, but rather its anti-dote. For survival means the better sides of our nature can eventually triumph. Not easily, not always, but often enough that our world can be improved. And perhaps one day, no war will be one of necessity, or survival.

—Jim DeFelice

Appendix A:

Timeline

═══════════

**MAJOR EVENTS IN WORLD WAR II
THAT AFFECTED HENRY**

_1939_
September—Germany invades Poland; Great Britain and France
   declare war

_1940_
April—Germany invades Norway and Denmark
May—Germany invades Belgium, Luxembourg, and the Nether-
   lands, then attacks France
May—Churchill becomes prime minister of Great Britain
June—Italy joins Germany, invading southern France
June—France surrenders to Germany
July—Germany begins regular bombing of England, initiating
   the air war known as the Battle of Britain
September—Jews in Germany are ordered to wear yellow stars
   on their clothes, making it easier to persecute them

September—The United States initiates the draft, part of a general mobilization

<u>1941</u>

February—German troops join Italian forces fighting the British in northern Africa

March—Roosevelt's plan to aid Britain, "Lend-Lease," is signed into law

May—German paratroopers assault Crete

June—Germany invades the Soviet Union

June—Mass executions of Jews in the occupied territories has begun

August—The United States and Great Britain announce the Atlantic Charter, summarizing goals for peace following the war

September—Though technically neutral, the United States escorts convoys across the Atlantic

December—Japan attacks Pearl Harbor

December—The United States declares war on Japan; Germany and Italy declare war on the United States

<u>1942</u>

January—German U-boats step up attacks on ships off the Atlantic seaboard

January—American troops arrive in Great Britain

April—German U-boats attack shipping in the Gulf Coast region

May—The last American troops in the Philippines surrender to Japan

June—The United States wins a major victory at Midway over the
Japanese fleet

June—The Manhattan Project begins, working on an atomic bomb

August—U.S. Army Rangers see action at Dieppe, France

September—The battle for Stalingrad begins in Russia, a major
turning point in the war on the Eastern Front

November—American troops land in Africa as part of Operation
Torch

1943

February—Shoe rationing begins in the United States

March—Losses by American troops in Africa lead to a change in
command, thrusting Patton and Bradley into key roles

**April—While still a high school senior, Henry enlists in the
Army as a paratrooper**

May—The Allies secure North Africa

July—Operation Husky, the invasion of Sicily, begins; paratroopers from the 82nd play a key role in the battle

August—Allied troops take control of Sicily

August—The 82nd Airborne is readied for a secret mission to land
in Rome in conjunction with an Italian surrender. The Italians
surrender, but the mission is never put into action.

September—The Allies invade Italy; the 82nd joins the fight, by
air and sea

September—The Pathfinder Concept, using highly skilled paratroopers to guide mass jumps, is conceived and used for the
first time

**Fall–early winter—Henry is trained as a paratrooper and dem-
olitions expert**

December—Most of the 82nd Airborne is moved to England to rest and restock. One regiment remains in Italy.

_1944_

January—Eisenhower arrives in England and begins planning the Normandy invasion

January—American troops land in Anzio, Italy

January—Henry completes airborne training

February—Henry ships out for Great Britain; he begins training for D-Day as soon as he arrives

April—Several hundred Allied troops training for D-Day die off Slapton Sands when their unarmed landing craft are attacked by German E-boats

June 4—Allied troops enter Rome

June 5/6—The 82nd and 101st Airborne Divisions jump into Normandy ahead of the seaborne D-Day forces

June 6—"D-Day"—the invasion of France—begins

June 7—After securing the beachheads, Allied forces begin to advance inland. The 82nd Airborne helps cut off the Cotentin Peninsula from the rest of France. Troops face the hedgerows for the first time.

June 19—Severe weather covers the Normandy area, hampering the Allied offensive and destroying one of the Mulberry artificial ports

June 26—Cherbourg is declared liberated, though a few small pockets of resistance remain

June 29—Henry is captured in a German counterattack in the bocage south of Saint-Sauveur-le-Vicomte

July—Critically wounded, Henry is taken to a hospital in

Paris. When he recovers, he is shipped eastward in a boxcar with other prisoners.

July—American forces break through the German lines near Saint-Lô in Operation Cobra

August—The American First and Third Armies race across France

August—Traveling mostly at night, Henry arrives outside a Nazi death camp. Though he and the other prisoners are convinced they will be killed there, they are eventually shipped to another camp.

August—Paris is liberated

September—Sometime this month, Henry begins working in a mine with other prisoners

September—The Allies reach Belgium and the Low Countries

October—The U.S. First Army occupies Aachen, the first sizable German city taken by the Americans

December—The Germans launch an offensive in the Ardennes, throwing Americans back in the Battle of the Bulge

_1945_

January—The American armies in the Bulge have regained the lost territory and renew their offensive toward Germany

March—Allied armies cross the Rhine

March—Henry escapes from the mines while being escorted back to the prison camp

April—Patton's Third Army drives across southern Germany

Early April—Henry meets a member of the U.S. Third Army, ending his ordeal

End of April/Early May—Henry returns home

May 8—VE Day: the war in Europe ends with a cease-fire at 00:01. Organized German resistance has ended.

July—Henry and his prewar sweetheart are married

August—America drops atomic bombs on Hiroshima and Nagasaki, effectively ending the war

August 15—VJ Day—the war is declared over, as the Allies accept Japan's unconditional surrender

September 2—The Japanese surrender documents are signed

Appendix B:

What They Carried

Aside from government-issued underwear, American paratroopers were equipped differently than other troops, and could be readily identified even when they weren't wearing their T-5 parachute and related paraphernalia.

Their special gear started with their jump jackets and pants, which had extra-large pockets, intended to hold extra ammo, food, and grenades, all necessary if you were spending two or three days behind enemy lines before being resupplied. Most D-Day paratroopers wore the M2 D-Bale Paratrooper Helmet, which had a liner, neckband, sweatband, and a wide chin cup and leather strap. (Though the helmet is generally associated with the invasion, not all paratroopers had the helmet on June 5, and some were issued to infantrymen as well.) The helmet was called the "D-bale" because of the D-shaped chin strap. The design was supposed to keep it from breaking during a jump.

The T-5 parachute was carried in a backpack, with straps around the torso. The T-5 opened with a hard jerk; when the chute deployed, the shock could be painful, especially if the strap happened to be slightly misaligned in the groin area. But as the saying goes: better to feel it than not.

U.S. paratroopers also carried a small reserve chute in a pouch at the front of their chests. While the main chute would be deployed by a static line attached to the aircraft during normal airborne operations, the reserve was activated by a handle at the front of the bag. Smaller, it was used only during emergencies; landings under the reserve tended to be much faster and harder than with the T-5.

Interestingly, the Americans were the only force that used reserves. The British decided having a backup would make a man lose confidence.

Paratroopers were equipped with a variety of weapons, depending on the date and their assignment. M-1 Garand rifles, the standard infantry rifle of the war, were usually broken down and carried in Griswold bags, quilted bags that were carried on the chest. Leg scabbards—basically very long holsters that were tied to the leg—were also sometimes used instead of the bags or a simpler rig across the chest.

The M-1 was the most common paratrooper weapon at the start of the war. Thompson submachine guns and, as the war progressed, the M-1 carbine, were also commonly used. A small number of paratroopers, designated as snipers or marksmen, carried Springfield bolt-action rifles in combat; these were generally considered more accurate than the M-1 and could be equipped with a scope.

The carbine, a lightweight .30-caliber semiautomatic, was especially popular with the troops; besides being lightweight, most had folding stocks, making them easier to jump with and carry. While it was "standard" to break down a long gun for a jump, arriving on the ground without a working rifle was not a palatable idea for many troopers, and many carried their weapons assembled, even when issued standard M-1s.

A musette bag with ammunition and (at times) spare underwear and toiletries was carried across the chest. Engineers like Henry also used the bags for blocks of TNT or plastic explosives.

A Mae West life jacket was worn over the reserve chute. Gas masks were carried on the D-Day jump, strapped to the left leg. On the right, a bayonet, with a jump knife in the boot. The jump knife was, usually, an M3 Trench Knife—a long-bladed weapon with a roped handle.

Webbing and the holster beneath the reserve held a .45 pistol, canteen, a shovel, first aid kit, and a bayonet. A long rope would also be carried, accessible so that it could be used to get down from a tree or a roof.

Other items, spread around in pockets or on the web where they could be secured, included a pocketknife, three days of rations, chocolate bars, grenades, compass, cigarettes, and ammunition, ammunition, ammunition—as much as they could cram in, which was never enough.

A raincoat, socks, handkerchiefs, and toilet paper—fifty sheets—were carried in a small field bag. Medical equipment included sulfur powder to disinfect wounds, two dressings, tape, and halazone tablets to purify water.

Appendix C:

The C-47

What was the most awesome American aircraft in World War II?

The B-17 Flying Fortress, bristling with machine guns, carrying upwards of 8,000 pounds of bombs, able to fly 2,000 miles or more?

The P-51 Mustang, with a top speed of 440 miles an hour, a range of 1,650 miles, and enough versatility to escort bombers deep into enemy territory or bust tanks with bombs, rockets, and six machine guns?

Here's a vote for the C-47, the unsung hero of World War II.

Officially the C-47 Skytrain, but also called the Dakota by British forces and the "Gooney Bird" by regular GIs, the C-47 was built by the Douglas Aircraft Company. It was based on the equally successful DC-3, which was introduced in 1936 and helped revolutionize commercial air travel. Some six hundred DC-3s were built; you could buy one for just under $80,000—roughly a million and a half dollars in today's money.

The DC-3 evolved from an earlier, smaller airliner, the DC-2, at a time when the aircraft travel by passengers was still novel and airlines made most of their money carrying freight and mail. The plane could hold thirty-two passengers, depending on its internal configuration, and was flown by a two-man crew. It cruised at 180 knots—a little over 200 miles per hour—with a service ceiling of 20,000 feet. It was powered by two Pratt & Whitney fourteen-cylinder engines; officially the R-1830 Twin Wasp, the radial, two-bank engine is legendary in its own right, said to be the most produced piston engine ever used in aviation, and surely one of the most dependable for its time.

Converting the DC-3 design to military use as the C-47 was not difficult. Most of the plane stayed the same, with the notable addition of a cargo door, a stronger floor, and an altered tail cone to allow the aircraft to tow gliders. An astrodome was installed to allow nighttime navigation with a sextant; a crew member would read the stars to plot (or stay on) a course.

The C-47's performance statistics remained roughly the same, though some Army statistics show the service could squeeze a few more knots out of the engines and another six thousand or so feet out of the service ceiling.

More than ten thousand C-47s in slightly different configurations were built during the war to transport troops and supplies to airstrips near the front lines. The Skytrain could use airfields that would strike fear into today's travelers; it was nothing to set down on an unmarked strip of grass, offload bales of supplies, and take off again—something that was done on the Normandy beachhead within hours of the landings. Officially, it needed 1,640 feet to land and could take off from 900. Pilots found ways to cut tens and even hundreds off those specs. The maximum payload was around 13,000 pounds; there was room for twenty-eight fully equipped soldiers. The interior was big enough to fit a Jeep.

A model of the plane, designated the C-53, was developed as a passenger-only aircraft; designation aside, there were only minor differences with the C-47, starting with the removal of the large cargo door. One variant, the C-53D Skytrooper, was used by paratroopers. Most troopers, however, flew in C-47s, as fewer than 160 of the C-53Ds were made.

C-47s served in the Pacific theater of operations as well as Europe, flying not only with the Allies but also with the Japanese—in the form of a license-built knockoff, the Showa and Nakajima L2D. Code-named "Tabby" by American intelligence, the aircraft looked very much like their American cousins, save for the large red sun on their fuselages and three more windows on each side of the cockpit. The Japanese versions were powered by Mitsubishi Kinsei engines, which delivered less horsepower in this application than the American Pratt & Whitney.

After the war, large numbers of surplus C-47s were sold to civilian airlines and individuals for a variety of uses. Some were still in service with the U.S. Air Force during the Vietnam War as transports and electronic warfare aircraft. In December 1964, a pair of C-47s with miniguns mounted in its rear door debuted in the Vietnam War as gunships. Able to stay aloft and circle a battlefield at low altitude, the planes' concentrated firepower proved to be devastating. Dubbed "Puff the Magic Dragon"—inspired by the first plane's call sign "Puff" and a reference to a popular song—the AC-47 became the mainstay of two newly created Air Commando Squadrons. Its success supporting ground troops led to further development of the type; today the role is filled by the AC-130, a specially built model of the C-130, itself a legendary cargo aircraft and worthy successor to the C-47.

Appendix D:

The "Mother" of Sainte-Mère-Église

────────────

The mayor of Sainte-Mère-Église had barely gotten to bed when the bell in the center of town began to peal. Someone knocked on the door of his pharmacy below.

"Fire!" the man in the street shouted. *"Feu!"*

Alexandre Renaud threw on some clothes and ran down to join the bucket brigade. His wife, Simone, roused by the commotion, checked on their three sons and then went out to the square. By the time she arrived, the flames were quite bright, illuminating not only the building on fire but the nearby church and the entire downtown area of the small Normandy village.

As the flames grew higher, a few of the townsmen threw nasty glances at the German soldiers who stood watching on the outskirts of the crowd. The occupiers were not popular in the town to begin with. They had flooded the nearby fields, destroying farmland and encouraging swarms of mosquitoes. Over the past several months, they had pressed locals into service preparing spiked and booby-trapped poles, which were planted orchard-like in fields. Both the flooding and the poles—Rommel's Asparagus, the locals called them—were intended to deter an attack by the Western Allies. It was doubly galling to not only be occupied, but to be made to actively work against any act of liberation.

Alexandre always pushed back against the Nazi requests, but there was only so much the World War I veteran could do. Badly wounded in that war and respected not only as the mayor but as the local druggist, Alexandre was beyond suspicion as a collaborator. Still, there was grumbling and discomfort.

Simone glanced away from the fire as a noise rose in the distance. The shouts from the crowd died off. The noise became a drone, then a roar—aircraft engines. Many of them.

Guns were firing. Antiaircraft batteries near the town.

What is going on?

The light of the fire threw odd patterns in the sky. Lollipops and circles—parachutes. Men descending quickly as the planes flew over.

Dozens of parachutes descended on the town. The German soldiers began reacting—shouting at first, then running in the direction of the falling men. Sharpshooters climbed into the church tower and began firing at the parachutists, both in the air and when they landed. One or more of the troopers were stuck on the spire.

The Germans shouted at the Frenchmen, ordering them back to their houses. While Simone went back upstairs to the children, the mayor went around to his garden and back out onto a side street to watch what was going on in secret. To his surprise, he found he was much closer to the action than he thought—a paratrooper crashed into a tree near his path, then fell with a splash into the flooded water on the other side of a stone wall. Alexandre reached over and helped the man out, pulling on the riser lines as the American soldier scrambled upward.

"I am French," the mayor told him when he got out. "Your friend."

The man thanked him, then disappeared.

Less than twelve hours later, the city would be under American control, the first sizable French town liberated on D-Day. The Nazi flag at the center of town had been torn down, replaced with an American flag; a few residents had joined the members of the 82nd Airborne in the grim task of collecting the bodies of the parachutists who'd been killed during or immediately after landing.

They were not the only deaths the citizens grieved—some thirty residents had been killed that night, caught in crossfires between the Germans and the Americans.

More was yet to come. The German troops outside the city attempted to throw the Americans back; the paratroopers fought to control not only the town but the nearby bridges and roads to the Utah beachhead. A stiff counterattack that afternoon prompted the French to seek shelter in a ditch on the east side of town. Simone and her children were there, hiding, when a friend came with her baby. Simone moved to give the woman and her child a seat; moments later, a mortar round exploded nearby, killing the friend.

The firefights nearby lasted several days, and it would take more than a month for the Allies to finally push their way past the German defenses and get off the Cotentin Peninsula, where Sainte-Mère-Église lay. It would take far longer for the town to rebuild itself.

Three cemeteries around the village were filled with Americans who had died during the Normandy campaign; just shy of 15,000 men. The number of men who had been killed stunned the local citizens; they marveled at the sacrifices people who lived a world away had made so that they could be free.

Simone walked regularly through the cemeteries, often planting flowers or otherwise tending to the fresh mounds. A photographer for *Life* magazine saw her and took some photos; one appeared in the magazine's August 1944 edition.

Almost immediately, the village began receiving letters asking about loved ones who had died in the battle. Some were addressed to Simone, some simply to the village or the mayor. Simone answered each one, telling what she knew of the graves, adding how brave the Americans had been, and mentioning how grateful the French were for their sacrifice. Often she would include petals of flowers.

And so began a lifetime of commemoration and consolation. Simone became known to the surviving relatives and friends of those who died in and around Sainte-Mère-Église as the Mother of Normandy. She tended to the graves religiously, answered letters nearly every day, and often was a tour guide for visitors in the decades following the war.

Simone passed away in 1988, but she has hardly been forgotten. A documentary on her life and efforts titled *Mother of Normandy— The Story of Simone Renaud* was released in 2010; it includes interviews with veterans from the battle as well as families and descendants of the townspeople.

Simone had a special level of energy and compassion, but her gratitude toward the American liberators was not unique among the French. In fact, it was and remains quite the opposite— monuments, plaques, and other memorials of the war are scattered liberally through the Normandy area commemorating the sacrifices of the Americans and others. Without noticeable exception, all are well cared for. American guests with even the slightest connection to the war are regularly honored in large and small ways. "Never forget" are not empty words there.

In 2018, Henry's son Dale took a trip to France, walking through much of the area where his father had fought. He spent time in Sainte-Mère-Église, where he was fortunate to meet one of Simone's sons, who graciously honored him and wrote a letter for his father, thanking him and all the soldiers he served with for their sacrifices.

Appendix E:

Combat Engineers

During the three and a half weeks he spent in Normandy, Henry essentially functioned as a "regular" paratrooper, a light, elite infantryman with special training in explosives. While not unique—he recalls there were at least six engineers with similar assignments attached to F company on the night of the invasion—on the whole, members of the Corps of Engineers remained with their native units, even when those units were given traditional infantry tasks, which occurred during the battle at La Fière bridge.

The Corps of Engineers that fought in Europe was the product of both evolution and revolution, and was a necessary part of a combat doctrine that called for high mobility, quick strikes, and coordination between what had been different branches of the Army—infantry, armor, artillery, and air. In order to stay mobile, an army needed bridges and highways; it needed airfields and supply lines. And it needed these constantly and instantly. It was no good to take one side of the Rhine, or any river, and then wait a few weeks or months until a captured bridge could be repaired or a new one built. The bridge had to be repaired or constructed as soon as possible, under fire if necessary. That was where combat engineers came in.

Less dramatic but equally important were airstrips, roads, port facilities—everything necessary to move and supply a massive army.

Following the Army's reorganization in the late 1930s, engineer battalions became part of each infantry and armored division. The battalions generally consisted of three companies in infantry divisions, and four in mechanized and armored divisions; one of these specialized in bridges. The engineer battalion also included a platoon of scouts.

Separately, a combat support regiment of engineers worked at the corps or army level, handling heavier tasks such as large river crossings. They were fighters, too; to survive in combat its inventory included twenty-four machine guns besides the trucks and dozers. More heavily equipped general engineer regiments, which had two battalions and support troops, handled large projects farther behind the lines. A separate regiment specialized in building airfields.

Companies of airborne engineers—like Henry's 307th—were fully airborne qualified. In Normandy, they were used in a number of ways. Clearing mines was arguably the most important, as the area had been heavily mined and booby-trapped. Engineers also set explosives to allow entry into buildings where German forces were holed up; while the difficulty of fighting through hedgerows has been written about extensively, machine-gun nests in the stone-walled houses on farms, hamlets, and villages were nearly as much of a barrier to the small units as they advanced.

Because they had also trained as infantry, combat engineer companies could be used on occasion as regular infantry. After helping secure the bridges in the first days of the invasion, companies from the 307th were tasked to provide security on some of them, even as other members of the unit made repairs elsewhere.

Some of the jobs the engineers did seem relatively mundane, or at least unexciting, to modern readers and even historians. But they were critical. Placing road signs that American forces could follow is probably the least appreciated task in a war zone . . . unless you happen to be a truck driver who got lost because he couldn't read French.

A total of 323,677 men were part of the engineer corps in Europe alone—a bit more than 10 percent of the total theater strength on VE Day. The percentage was even higher in the Pacific. While the bulk of these men usually worked behind the lines, it was not a safe job, especially for the combat companies integrated with frontline divisions. The 307th lost more than a hundred men during the course of the war, twenty-one in Normandy alone. Thirty-two men besides Henry were taken prisoner; six men remain listed in the company rolls as MIA.

Appendix F:

Americans in Concentration Camps

―――――――
―――――――

By the late 1960s, American animosity toward Germany had faded to the point that even POW camps could be portrayed lightly as comic palaces, as they were in *Hogan's Heroes*, a highly successful sitcom that ran from September 1965 to April 1971 on CBS, and was one of the country's most-watched shows during the first years of its run.

While the point of the show was mostly to lampoon the Nazis, camp life in the Stalag seemed terribly sweet and downright creative. The prisoners looked well fed and even well dressed. Work details were welcomed as an excuse to prepare for commando raids perpetrated by the prisoners, and there was always room in the tunnels below the camp to hide one more spy en route to England with top secret information.

The reality, as Henry's story shows, was far different. Rations in even the best camps for officers—almost always a cut above those for enlisted POWs—were meager, even at the height of Germany's ascendancy. At Oflag 64, for example, where George Patton's son-in-law John Waters was imprisoned, prisoners got perhaps an ounce of meat and a few ounces of vegetables and bread a day. Goods from the Red Cross, when they arrived, were often damaged. Security was lax enough that the prisoners could build and hide a secret radio and listen to BBC broadcasts—but there was little chance of escape, and anyone trying would be dealt with harshly.

At the other extreme, a small number of POWs were held at concentration camps—not, like Henry, for only a few days, but for the duration of their imprisonment.

As detailed by Flint Whitlock in his book *Given Up for Dead*, and Roger Cohen in *Soldiers and Slaves*, a number of soldiers captured during the Battle of the Bulge were marched and transported by train to the town of Bad Orb, Germany, arriving there on December 1944. The conditions of their trip mirrored those Henry experienced, with two exceptions—the trip was somewhat shorter, but far colder, as they were traveling through the frigid winter rather than the hot summer. Marching past Christmas decorations in town, ducking snowballs thrown by the locals, and pushed on by dogs as well as guards, the soldiers were led to Stalag IX-B, a prison camp separated by woods from the town.

The camp had housed prisoners since the invasion of Poland in 1939. Life there was dismal, typical of most Stalags. Fail to salute a German officer or say something that could be considered an insult by someone who didn't even speak your language, and you were liable to be beaten. Boredom was a constant companion, and the Geneva Convention might just as well have been a chapter in Grimm's fairy tales. But in the context of German POW camps, it was no worse than many.

On January 18, 1945, the American prisoners at Stalag IX-B who were Jewish were ordered to assemble the next morning. (The

German administration seems to have overlooked the fact that the men's dog tags were stamped with letters signifying their faith, or perhaps they reserved that as a last resort if the men did not volunteer.)

The first day, everyone refused. But a large contingent of heavily armed German soldiers the next morning convinced most of the Jewish soldiers to identify themselves to spare their comrades of retribution. Somewhere between eighty and one hundred Americans were taken from the barracks and put into a separate area of the camp. Harder work details were assigned. They had trouble obtaining enough firewood for their single source of heat, a potbellied stove—even though they were cutting the wood themselves.

In February, the segregated prisoners, along with another 250 prisoners from the main area of the camp, were told they were going to a new camp. They were marched back to the trains and transported to Berga.

Berga was a satellite work camp of Buchenwald, one of the most notorious Nazi extermination and concentration camps.

While Buchenwald was one specific place, it was much larger in a sense, with well over a hundred smaller camps affiliated with it in various ways, a kind of conglomerate of death. Berga itself had two camps, a large one for political prisoners and another that was used to house the POWs. Confined to five shacks on a barbed-wire enclosed hilltop, they were crowded together in conditions even worse than IX-B. They were assigned to help the political prisoners dig shafts for bomb shelters in a nearby mountain.

About a thousand political prisoners were already working on the shafts. Emaciated, sick, the men worked only to avoid being beaten by foremen—other political prisoners, possibly rewarded with a little food and undoubtedly motivated by threats from the Germans.

The Americans worked in twelve-hour shifts, alternating with the prisoners.

In March, conditions became even worse after the camp commandant was replaced by a sergeant in the home guard. (While most if not all of the guards at Berga One and those who escorted the Americans to the shafts seem to have all been SS, the new commandant was not.) Political prisoners were hanged almost daily; the guards made sure the Americans marched past them as they went to work. A few prisoners tried to escape; nearly all were captured. Most of these men were beaten and given harder work details and deprived of food; a few were shot and then displayed as examples.

The Red Cross apparently knew about Berga; the surviving inmates spoke of a "visit" by a representative at one point during the winter. But while this meant that there was a possibility of mail and even inspections, the POWs remained isolated without communication with the outside world, and no hope of anything but more slave labor.

Disease, overwork, and malnutrition killed many of the men. In late March, the Americans were moved to a large building near Berga One, the political prisoner camp closer to town. They also received a new work assignment, felling logs in the forest rather than working on the tunnel. A few Red Cross packages began to arrive.

The men had no idea what was going on, but you don't have to be too cynical to realize that the Germans, either at the camp or above, had realized that the war was going badly and that restitution would be in the offing when the Allies arrived.

That happened April 2. Most of the guards had fled during the night.

The former commandant was put on trial for war crimes at the camp, convicted, and sentenced to death. But the sentence was reduced following his appeal. Released in the mid-1950s, he found a job and faded into the fabric of his community.

Appendix G:

Encouraging Escapes

Very few POWs attempted to escape, and only a comparative handful managed to survive. The most famous escape was documented by Paul Brickhill in the book *The Great Escape*. A total of seventy-six men escaped from a tunnel dug under the fence at Stalag III before the seventy-seventh was seen coming up out of the ground by a guard. Seventy-three of the men were caught; fifty were arbitrarily chosen to be shot.

Two men made it to Switzerland, which was neutral during the war; a third was helped by French Resistance and reached the British consulate in Spain, also officially neutral though politically aligned with the Nazis. A highly fictionalized version of the escape (though based on the nonfiction and accurate book) starring Steve McQueen, James Garner, and Richard Attenborough was released in 1963; it was one of the highest-grossing films of the year.

Given that German prison camps were located deep within enemy-held territory, generally in Germany or Poland, escape was impractical if not impossible. But a secret U.S. War Department unit worked to encourage prisoners to escape nonetheless.

Called MIS-X, the agency adopted some of the techniques of the British MI-9 branch, known as the British Prisoner of War Branch. Among other things, MI-9 created relief agencies that sent packages to imprisoned soldiers. Inside the packages were items that could help escapees. These might include anything from a compass or a hidden map to a saw that could cut through metal.

Established in October 1942, the MIS-X was started with a tiny budget—$25,000. It created a fake charity and began putting packages together that contained items like a phony game board that could be steamed open to reveal maps or other papers that would help an escapee.

While at least some of their packages are known to have been intercepted, MIS-X succeeded in communicating with a handful of prisoners, receiving coded messages back. A plot possibly aided by MIS-X at a camp in German-allied Romania was detected or betrayed. Two radios and cameras made it into Stalag VII-A, Mosberg, Germany; a prisoner there sent coded messages back to the Allies whenever possible.

It was believed during the war that prisoners gained morale if they were actively working to escape. Even if that was so—and conditions inside the camps surely had the most impact on morale by far—how much of an effect the project had on morale is impossible to determine.

Appendix H:

The Toll

———————

Estimates of the total number of people killed in World War II vary, ranging as high as 85 million, counting civilians and those killed in the Holocaust.

The American military lost more than 400,000, mostly men, during the war, the vast majority to enemy action.

According to the National Archives, just over one hundred of Henry's friends and neighbors in Clinton County, Iowa, were killed during the war. This is the official list:

Clinton County, Iowa, List of WWII Soldiers

Claud Adamson, PFC

Maurice B. Allender, S. SG

Victor G. Anderson, Tec4

Louis H. Baker, PVT

William R. Barber, PVT

Allen J. Bark, PVT

Alvin L. Berding, SGT

Melvin C. Bitker, PVT

Laurence L. Boekeloo, CPL

Jack C. Boysen, Tec5

Marcus S. Brough, PVT

Donald J. Brown, PFC

Edward Bruggenwirth, PFC

Clyde C. Bunce, PFC

Donald T. Burke, 2 LT

John E. Burke, 2 LT

Lavern P. Busch, 2 LT

David W. Byers, PFC

George E. Carr, PVT

Theodore F. Chase, TEC5

John W. Clark, PVT

Marvin A. Clark, PVT

Reynold J. Connole, PFC

William F. Cooper, PVT

France T. Dolan, TEC5

Leroy L. Dreyer, PFC

Roy A. Dunmore, PVT

Irvin F. Ehlers, PFC

Harvey R. Fatchett, PVT

Wilber Finkboner, PVT

Lyle E. Fromang, PVT

Albert C. Fugate, PFC

Dean E. Fuller, PFC

Norbert J. Grandick, S SG

Cyril H. Gustavison, PFC

Leon T. Hanson, PFC

Cyril G. Heineman, S SG

Louis V. Heienman, PFC

Louis W. Heineman, PFC

Robert L. Hendricks, TEC4

Edward W. Holle, Jr., PFC

Robert J. Holliday, TEC5

Robert L. Janica, PVT

Aaron A. Kenyon, 1 LT

Herbert A. Koch, PVT

Robert F. Krayenhagen, PFC

Lee B. Lampe, PVT

Vernon E. Laschanzky, 2 LT

Donald W. Lass, PVT

Raymond H. Lenson, T SG

Dale R. Leonard, PVT

Ray W. Magin, S SG

Henry E. Mangelsen, PFC

Daniel Manley, CAPT

Elmer T. McClain, PFC

Laurence P. McKenna, T SG

John R. Meader, Jr., 2 LT

Darwin F. Michaelsen, 2 LT

Frank Milota, Jr., PVT

Roger M. Mull, T SG

Marvin H. Munson, PFC

Laurence R. Naeve, PVT

William A. Nelson, PVT

Harold H. Otto, PVT

Roy E. Paulsen, Jr., PVT

Gilbert C. Penzkofer, PFC

James B. Piatt, SGT

Louis L. Pool, PFC

Henry Raap, SGT

Philip L. Ray, CPL

Raymond H. Rehr, PFC

Herbert L. Reisinger, PVT

Hampton E. Rich, 1 LT

Elmer J. Roe, PVT

Robert B. Ryner, S SG

George E. Sander, PVT

Earl E. Schmidt, 1 LT

Roy P. Schmidt, PFC

Aubrey C. Serfling, CAPT

Louis H. Simpson, S SG

Frank J. Sirvid, S SG

Kenneth C. Sivertsen, SGT

William L. Slowie, PVT

James A. Soesbe, 2 LT

Elmer W. Stahl, PFC

Ernie E. Stamp, S SG

Urban P. Stodden, PFC

Herbert O. Stoecker, SGT

Gerald F. Stoltenberg TEC5

Albert L. Strohn, 2 LT

Frank A. Swanson, CAPT

Donald D. Thess, PFC

Cleo E. Thomas, T SG

Frederick A. Thompson, SGT

Mearl L. Toerber, PFC

James F. Torpey, PFC

Francis E. Web, PVT
Virgil H. White, M SG
Clarence A. Wright, 1 LT
Robert T. Yegge, PVT
Gerald M. Zimmerman, SGT

Appendix I:

What It Took—Factory Production

The massive armada necessary to land thousands of men in France in June 1944 impressed everyone who was part of it. Henry marveled at the number of ships he glimpsed from the aircraft as he rode toward France; other witnesses have said there were so many vessels it looked as if one could simply walk across them to the distant shore.

Where did all of these come from?

American factories primarily.

It is both truthful and a cliché that U.S. production was a critical factor in the war. Not only did the country supply American troops, but both Great Britain and the Soviet Union relied on American arms and goods as well.

Some numbers: In 1939, America's gross national product—the sum of all goods produced—was $88,600,000. By 1944, the GNP was $135,000,000 (valued in the worth of 1939 dollars). War production was 2 percent of total output in 1939; by 1943, it was 40 percent. It's true, also, that civilians benefited to some degree from the increase in production that came from war goods; consumer purchases increased by 12 percent between 1939 and 1944, despite rationing and severe shortages. But large consumer items, like refrigerators and washing machines, were in tight supply; even after the war, Henry's family simply couldn't find a refrigerator to buy.

The economic expansion caused by the war was the greatest in American history; it may have been the greatest ever in the modern era. Industrial production grew at about 15 percent a year, compared to 7 percent during World War I, itself a period of rapid growth. Increased productivity, and not just the diversion of resources to the war effort, helped account for much of the boom.

The switch-over from civilian to war production by large companies like General Motors greatly aided the war effort, but small factories—including the one in Clinton, Iowa, where Arlene worked—made the switch as well. The boom was felt at all levels of industry. Machine tools, often produced by relatively small firms, increased by a factor of six from 1939 to 1942, the peak of the increase.

Some of the effects of the wartime economy continued after the war, most obviously in the influx of women in the workplace. Many women gave up full-time jobs when the war ended and the "boys" returned home, but a significant number stayed, setting the stage for a dramatic change in society. Technological advances made during the war in any number of fields reached the civilian market soon after. To take a very obvious one: civilian jet aircraft, nonexistent in 1939, began dominating air traffic in the 1950s, soon after the introduction of the first jet airliner, the British de Haviland Comet, in regular flights in 1952. Surely many innovations would have come eventually, but the war speeded them up.

Besides the direct effects on the economy, the war set the stage for a new era in trade between nations. The Atlantic Charter announced between Roosevelt and Churchill in 1941 spoke of reducing trade restrictions; both the United States and Great Britain began working toward that goal when hostilities concluded. The determination to rebuild not just the shattered Allied nations but also Germany and Japan—a reaction to one of the perceived causes of Hitler's rise—also made for a very different world economy in the postwar era.

While these were nationwide and international effects of the war, it took individuals to make it all happen. Working longer hours, sacrificing individual luxuries in the name of a common goal—all of this occurred while families were under the strain of missing family members. There were other stresses as well. While the North American continent proved too distant from Japan, Germany, and Italy to suffer sustained attacks like the London Blitz, many Americans on the coasts nonetheless feared for their safety. At least in the beginning stages of the war, air raid drills were not a joke.

All of this raises the question: *Could the country make such sacrifices today?*

Many veterans of the war, including Henry, have their doubts. In Henry's view, the Great Depression helped the country in a subtle way, preparing people for the hardships war imposes.

Fortunately, the years that followed World War II have not called for similar sacrifices. With the loss of people who lived through the war years and the spirit they engendered, the collective memory of the cooperation and sacrifices may diminish. One of Henry's goals in telling his story was to keep some of that memory, and perhaps that collective spirit, alive.

Appendix J:

Further Reading

—————

When we began working on this book, we'd heard there were less than a thousand men still alive who had fought on D-Day and in the Normandy battles. That number has surely dwindled. Part of our goal therefore has been to keep the memory of those men as well as the war alive; toward that end, we hope and trust that readers will want to seek out more information in other venues.

There is no substitute for actually visiting the beaches and surrounding area, including Sainte-Mère-Église and the invasion beaches in France. D-Day and World War II are very much alive there, in countless museums, historical monuments, and plaques. American visitors are often overcome with emotion at the respect and gratitude the French still show toward the soldiers who made the ultimate sacrifice freeing them more than seventy-five years ago.

In the United States, the National World War II Museum in New Orleans has artifacts, information, and programs on all aspects of the war; it's especially deep in the area of D-Day. The website: https://www.nationalww2museum.org/.

The National D-Day Memorial in Bedford, Virginia, is an inspiring memorial to the soldiers who fought on the beaches and often features programs with surviving World War II veterans. Bedford and the surrounding area was the home of many of the members of the 116th Infantry Regiment, a National Guard unit that was part of the 29th Infantry, which landed at Omaha, and much of the information at the memorial is related to the 29th, but the displays and memorial are universal. The website: https://www.dday.org/.

Immediately following the war, the U.S. Army produced an official history of operations; currently available online, it remains an accessible and informative introduction for general readers. A general readers' guide to these volumes and others associated with World War II can be found at https://history.army.mil/books/wwii/11-9/11-9c.htm.

There are countless books, movies, and videos on the war and D-Day in particular. Here are a few that are accessible to readers without a deep background in the war's history. Rick Atkinson's best-selling Liberation Trilogy follows the American army through the European Theater. The first book, *An Army at Dawn*, details the North Africa campaign. *The Day of Battle* details Sicily and the fight in Italy. *The Guns at Last Light* take the reader through Normandy, France, and into the end of the war in Germany. *Mighty Endeavor* by Charles B. MacDonald is an older book that covers the same ground in one volume. Andrew Roberts's *The Storm of War* is a one-volume history of the entire war.

Among the multitude of books about D-Day, Stephen Ambrose's *D Day: June 6, 1944: The Climactic Battle of World War II*; *Overlord* by Max Hastings; and the longer *D-Day: The Battle for Normandy* by Antony Beevor stand out.

Though older than the others, *The Longest Day* by Cornelius Ryan is another great one-volume read. A 1957 film version is considered one of the greatest war films of all time. The more recent *Saving Private Ryan*, while fictional, includes scenes of the D-Day landing at Utah Beach that many veterans consider highly realistic.

For readers interested in a thorough history of the 82nd Division's action in the war, there is no substitute for Phil Nordyke's two-volume set, *All American, All the Way*.

A fine account of the role of Pathfinders during Normandy and beyond is included in *First to Jump* by Jerome Preisler.

Notes

CHAPTER 1: MIDDLE AMERICA

Some of the information about Clinton and its history comes from *Images of America: Clinton, Iowa,* by the Clinton County Historical Society.

While Merchant Marine sailors could earn more than soldiers and sailors in the armed forces, they did not receive the benefits servicemen were entitled to. They were paid only for the time they were working—which meant that if their ship went down, the time they spent in the lifeboat, if they were lucky enough to get to one, was unpaid. Their income could also be taxed; service income could not.

According to a study done by the War Shipping Administration, a seaman first class in the Navy made only $11 less after taxes per year than the equivalent in the Merchant Marine; a Navy petty officer second class made about $176 a year more. The value of insurance against disability and injuries tipped the salary balance far in favor of service members, even before the introduction of the GI Bill and its benefits in 1944. Some details of the study are available on the U.S. merchant marine site at http://www.usmm.org/salary.html.

There is some disagreement between historians about the actual number of casualties, but it is generally believed that more than seven hundred merchant ships were sunk during the war, with over 8,000 sailors losing their lives in the service. Other casualties, including men captured as POWs, are thought to have topped 13,000. Nonetheless, during and after the war the sailors were often looked down upon by the population at large.

Data on industrial and trade production come from statistics kept by the Federal Reserve Bank of St. Louis, known colloquially as "Fred"; see for example the Index of Industrial Production and Trade for United States (M1204CUSM363SNBR).

CHAPTER 2: TRAINING UP

Some of the information on the *Queen Elizabeth*'s background comes from John Shepherd's history at liverpoolships.org: http://www.liver poolships.org/the_cunard_white_star_liner_queen_elizabeth.html.

And the WWII Database entry by Alan Chanter: https://ww2db .com/other.php?other_id=44.

Estimates of the number of passengers carried by the *Queen Elizabeth* during the war vary. According to Shepherd, *Elizabeth* made thirty-five trips from April 1941 to March 1945, carrying over 800,000 passengers. Her sister ship, the *Queen Mary*, is said to have held the record for the number of passengers taken on a single voyage at 16,683, topping *Elizabeth*'s best of 15,932 by nearly a thousand. The summer trips typically carried more men.

While Henry wrote home to his parents and Arlene often, only two letters seem to have survived; both are reproduced in this chapter. The letters here have been lightly edited.

Population numbers come from the census; the numbers of service people come from the National World War II Museum.

CHAPTER 3: JUNE 1944

Before Roosevelt, exactly three Democratic presidential candidates had carried Iowa since it had won statehood: Cass in 1848, Pierce in 1852, and Woodrow Wilson in 1912. Both Pierce and Wilson were elected.

The quote "full of menace" comes from J. M. Stagg, *Forecast for Overlord*. Group Captain Stagg was an RAF meteorologist tasked with advising Eisenhower. He was assisted by both American and British meteorologists, who did not always agree.

The quote from Gavin's speech, which was delivered to the 508th, comes from an account by paratrooper Edward Boccafoglio, archived at the National World War II Museum in New Orleans.

Some sources indicate that C-53s were used in the air assault by the 82nd Airborne. Essentially an improved model of the C-47, the aircraft differed from its sister ship in only a few significant ways, including the lack of a large door for loading and offloading cargo. A little under four hundred were produced—a sizable number to be sure, but relatively small compared to the output of the C-47, which was considered more versatile because of its cargo door and other factors.

Henry's memory is that his plane and those around him were all C-47s, which agrees with the records we have at hand.

CHAPTER 4: DROP ZONE

Though not on the same scale as the invasion of Crete, the Germans considered the airborne operations in Holland their first massed use of airborne troops.

The battles the first night and days afterward were extremely confusing for both sides, something that is reflected in the firsthand accounts and after-battle reports. As a baseline for sorting them, we have relied on *Four Stars of Valor*, by Phil Nordyke, which seems the best-organized overall account.

Four soldiers from the 82nd received the Congressional Medal of Honor in World War II: Private John R. Towle, Private First Class Charles N. DeGlopper, First Sergeant Leonard A. Funk, Jr., and Private Joe Gandara. Two other soldiers, Lieutenant Colonel Emory J. Pike and Corporal Alvin C. York, received the medal for action in World War I. Staff Sergeant Félix Modesto Conde Falcón was accorded the honor during the Vietnam War.

In *The Longest Day*, Cornelius Ryan mentions an officer saying that he had heard of a Canadian paratrooper coming through a greenhouse roof in their sector. The incident was highly fictionalized in the movie based on the book.

Regarding the battle at La Fière: some historians contend that the Germans regained full control of the bridge after June 6, a point bitterly contended by some of the veterans of the fight. Henry was not an eyewitness to the frontline fighting, but his recollection is that the Germans did not succeed in pushing the Americans back once they had a foothold. The fact that he and the men he was with were not called up to the line would seem to back the contention of the veterans of the fight.

While to this day Henry marvels over his brief encounter with General Gavin and what he said, a number of other GIs reported similar encounters.

CHAPTER 5: HEDGEROWS

In terms of bomb tonnage and even casualties, the V-1 attacks were relatively insignificant compared to the damage done in the earlier Blitz, to say nothing of American and British bombing missions on German cities. A good portion of Allied bombs fell inadvertently on civilians, and there were also raids that deliberately targeted civilian areas, such as (most famously) Dresden.

However, the psychological effect of the V-1 attacks was significant. Some estimates say that a million people left the London area because of the attacks, damaging the war effort by depriving the city of workers.

The Pyle quote is from *Brave Men*. It is also quoted and discussed in depth by James Holland in *Normandy '44: D-Day and the Epic 77-Day Battle for France*.

CHAPTER 6: PRISONER

As explained in the text, Henry was told that the death camp where he was kept was Auschwitz. This is plausible. The rail lines to Poland were still open and American prisoners were being kept in Poland in the summer of 1944. It's possible that the Germans intended to inter him at a Polish camp, but changed plans for some reason. But we could find no documentation to show the basis for that statement.

Henry's description of the train yard and the bombing attack would not fit in with the main camp at Auschwitz, and we believe based on that and other research that it is far more likely that the death camp was in Germany, closer to the mines where he was put to work. However, we cannot rule out Auschwitz, and the lack of documentation does not prove anything one way or the other.

Henry's prisoner of war records at the National Archive erroneously indicate that he was captured on June 6, 1944, and that he was interned at Stalag 13B in Welden, Bavaria; a notation indicates that the information on the camp came from an outside source, rather than the U.S. Army.

The general description of Stalag 13 matches Henry's memory, as do some of the circumstances, such as the proximity of the mines and the presence of Russian prisoners.

Henry believes that he was sent to a Stalag 12, based on his recollection of seeing a sign with that designation, Stalag XII, upon entering the camp, and what he was told by Army personnel later. That is the only designation he was aware of, until we started working on this book. The designation would place the camp in Saxony, a good distance from Welden, and in an area where there were also a large number of work camps. Stalag 12A was used as a processing center for enlisted personnel, which would also align with his memories.

Based on our research and Henry's memory, we believe that it is likely he was at 12A, processed, and then sent to a work camp and mine. That possibly was 13B, but it would seem more likely that it was a Buchenwald concentration camp satellite administered by the SS, and that the camp notation is simply incorrect. It is also possible that his memory is faulty, or the notations are related to an administrative arrangement by the Germans that obscured the fact that he was at a concentration camp.

The German system of designating prison camps can be confusing. Patton's son-in-law, Lieutenant Colonel John Waters, was imprisoned at Oflag XIII-B in February 1945 after being held in Poland. Though the designation makes it seem as if it was related to Henry's, it was located 120 miles to the north, near Hammelburg. "Oflag" indicated that it was a camp for officers, who were usually housed in a different camp than enlisted personnel. The Germans had different camps for different nationalities as well as enlisted and officers. Captured airmen were usually held in camps run by the Luftwaffe, separately from ground soldiers.

CHAPTER 7: THE MINES

The Geneva Convention is available online at https://ihl-databases.icrc.org/applic/ihl/ihl.nsf/INTRO/305?OpenDocument.

CHAPTER 8: THE WAR OUTSIDE THE FENCE

Statistics on the number of MIAs and POWs are taken from the paper "Former American Prisoners Of War (POWs)," Office of the Assistant Secretary for Policy, Planning, and Preparedness (OPP&P), by Robert E. Klein, Ph.D., Office of the Actuary, OPP&P, Michael R. Wells, M.S., Office of Data Management and Analysis, OPP&P, and Janet Somers, B.A., Office of Data Management and Analysis, OPP&P, published in April 2005.

The battles at the Falaise Pocket—and especially the Allies' failure to close the gap at the east—have been a matter for great debate among historians, armchair and otherwise. Whether the Allied commanders were ultimately prudent or overly cautious, the fact remains that a large portion of the German army was killed or lost its heavy equipment as they left the pocket.

Bradley's sentiments about bombing German cities along the way were included in the contemporaneous journal kept by his aide Chet Hansen. While not necessarily out of character, they were unusually direct in addressing civilian targets. For the most part, Hansen's notes don't show Bradley directly referring to collateral damage or what amount to acts of revenge.

Most historians blame the failure of the MarketGarden operation on two factors: first, and overwhelmingly, the air plan was insufficient; not enough forces and supplies could be mustered to take Arnhem, or to hold the areas in general. Second, the failure to quickly take Nijmegen meant that the British could not be reinforced or resupplied from the ground. It also made it much easier for the Germans to defend Arnhem and the bridge there.

CHAPTER 10: WHAT HAD TO BE DONE

After all these years, there is no way to independently research and verify the events Henry describes in Chapter 10. He is convinced that he killed the individuals mentioned in the narrative, and admits struggling with his conscience over the incidents.

CHAPTER 11: HOME

The Patton letter is reprinted on page 660 of *The Patton Papers*, edited by Martin Blumenson, first DaCapo edition, 1996.

APPENDICES

Much of the information about Simone Renaud is drawn from the book *Mother of Normandy*, by Jeff Stoffer, a companion to the documentary of the same name. Additional information is from the book *Sainte-Mère-Église D-Day, June 6th 1944*, by Alexandre Renaud, her son.

The information on Waters's diet comes from Rick Atkinson, *The Guns at Last Light*, which cites Waters's handwritten log.

As noted in the text, much of the information about the prisoners at Berga Two comes from books by Roger Cohen and Flint Whitlock. Cohen especially argues that the two men prosecuted for crimes at Berga Two were treated with leniency because of geopolitical considerations.

Some of the information on MIS-X comes from Lloyd R. Shoemaker's book *The Escape Factory*. The book is one of the few secondary sources detailing MIS-X's efforts. The bulk of the agency's original records are said to have been destroyed immediately after the war.

Some of the information on the Engineers comes from Peter Turnbull, *"I Maintain the Right"—The 307th Airborne Engineer Battalion in WWII*, and Alfred M. Beck et al., *The Corps of Engineers*.

The numbers related to war production are quoted from charts in Alan S. Milward's *War, Economy and Society 1939–1945*, a thorough economic analysis of the war at the macroeconomic level.

Acknowledgments

This book could not have been written without the support and efforts of the entire Langrehr family, most especially Henry and Arlene's daughter Kay, who was a tremendous help not only by gathering materials and keeping us on schedule but also by whipping up food at various points to keep energy levels up.

Thanks also to our friends at First Army, who first introduced us.

Debra Scacciaferro provided background research and editorial assistance, as well as helpful suggestions on several aspects of the text.

At William Morrow, Peter Hubbard and Nick "Cadillac" Amphlett provided valuable notes, feedback, and constant encouragement.

The primary sources for this book are a series of interviews and conversations between Henry and Jim beginning in the summer of 2019 and extending to early 2020, including several days' worth of intensive formal interviews conducted at Henry's house in Clinton, Iowa, in November 2019, where Arlene joined and provided valuable information and prompts.

Additional family sources and earlier interviews, including a taped speech and a one-hundred-plus-page handwritten reminiscence by Henry in 1994–95, were also critical.

A large number of news organizations have interviewed Henry over the years; those accounts were also valuable as background material.

At times, there were small conflicts between the different accounts Henry has given over the years. If the conflict could not be logically resolved with the help of documentation or outside accounts, more weight was generally given to the earlier version. In cases where we could not immediately verify certain incidents, we have omitted them. Major conflicts and possible errors are noted in the text and notes.

Additional resources and secondary sources included the following:

National Archives

U.S. Army After Action Reports—307th Airborne Engineer Battalion

Supreme Headquarters Allied Expeditionary Force Evaluation and Dissemination Section, *German Concentration Camps*, May 1945

The official U.S. Army History of the war, United States Army in World War II, CMH Publication 11-9, Center of Military History, United States Army, Washington, D.C., 1992. Available online at https://history.army.mil/html/bookshelves/resmat/ww2eamet.html.

Rick Atkinson, *The Day of Battle—The War in Sicily and Italy, 1943–1944*, Henry Holt, 2007.

Rick Atkinson, *The Guns at Last Light—The War in Western Europe, 1944–1945*, Henry Holt, 2013.

Mitchell G. Bard, *Forgotten Victims: The Abandonment of Americans in Hitler's Camps*, Westview Press, 1994.

Alfred M. Beck et al., *The Corps of Engineers: The War Against Germany*, U.S. Army, 1988.

Anthony Beevor, *D-Day, The Battle for Normandy*, Viking, 2009.

Roger E. Bilstein, *Airlift and Airborne Operations in World War II*. Air Force History and Museum Program, 1998

Martin Blumenson, *The Patton Papers—1940–1945*, DaCapo Press, 1996.

T. Michael Booth and Duncan Spencer, *Paratrooper—The Life of Gen. James M. Gavin*, Simon & Schuster, 1994.

Roland Charles, *Troopships of World War II*, Army Transport Association, April 1947.

Clinton County Historical Society, *Clinton, Iowa*, Arcadia, 2003.

Roger Cohen, *Soldiers and Slaves*, Knopf, 2005.

Branch D. Coll, *The Corps of Engineers: Troops and Equipment*, U.S. Army, 1988.

Napier Crookenden, *Dropzone Normandy*, Charles Scribner & Sons, 1976.

George Forty, *Patton's Third Army at War*, Scribner, 1978.

James Jay Garafano, *After D-Day: Operation Cobra and the Normandy Breakout*, Lynne Rienner, 2000.

Kent Roberts Greenfield et al., *The Organization of Ground Combat Troops*, Historical Division of the Army, 1947.

Franz Halder et al., *Airborne Operations, A German Appraisal*, U.S. Army (CMH Pub 104-13).

James Holland, *Normandy '44*, Atlantic Monthly Press, 2019.

Bernd Horn and Michel Wyczynski, "A Most Irrevocable Step:

Canadian Paratroopers on D-Day, The first 24 hours, 5–6 June 1944," Canadian Military History: Vol. 13: Iss. 3, Article 3. Available at: http://scholars.wlu.ca/cmh/vol13/iss3/3

Orr Kelly, *Meeting the Fox*, John Wiley & Sons, 2002.

David M. Kennedy, editor, *The Library of Congress World War II Companion*, Simon & Schuster, 2007.

Charles B. MacDonald, *Mighty Endeavor—The American War in Europe*, William Morrow, 1986.

Leo Marriott and Simon Forty, *The Normandy Battlefields*, Casemate, 2014.

Charles Messenger, *The D-Day Atlas*, Thames & Hudson, 2014.

Alan S. Milward, *War, Economy and Society 1939–1945*, University of California Press, 1979.

Robert M. Murphy, *No Better to Die*, Casemate, 2011.

Phil Nordyke, *All American, All the Way—From Market Garden to Berlin*, Zenith Press, 2005.

Phil Nordyke, *All American, All the Way—From Sicily to Normandy*, Zenith Press, 2005.

Phil Nordyke, *Four Stars of Valor*, Zenith Press, 2006.

Jerome Preisler, *First to Jump*, Da Capo, 2017.

Alexandre Renaud, *Sainte-Mère-Église, D-Day, June 6th 1944*, Maurice Renard, 2014 (reprinted from a 1945 edition).

Lloyd R. Shoemaker, *The Escape Factory*, St. Martin's, 1990.

Colonel Roy M. Stanley II, *The Normandy Invasion*, Pen & Sword Military (no publishing date listed).

Jeff Stoffer, *Mother of Normandy*, Iron Mike Entertainment, 2010.

Peter Turnbull, *"I Maintain the Right"—The 307th Airborne Engineer Battalion in WWII*, AuthorHouse, 2005.

Flint Whitlock, *Given Up for Dead: American GI's in the Nazi Concentration Camp at Berga*, Westview Press, 2005.

Photo Insert Credits

Page 1, top; page 6, top; page 7, top; page 7, bottom; page 8, top; page 8, bottom; page 11, top; page 14, top: U.S. Army.

Page 1, bottom; page 4, top: U.S. Air Force.

Page 2, top; page 2, bottom; page 5; page 9, bottom right; page 10, top right; page 10, bottom; page 13, top; page 13, bottom; page 15; page 16: Courtesy of the authors.

Page 3, top left; page 3, top right; page 3, bottom; page 10, top left: National Archives.

Page 4, bottom: Adrian Pingstone.

Page 6, bottom; page 11, bottom: Imperial War Museums.

Page 9, top: Jebulon.

Page 12, top: Bundesarchiv.

Page 12, bottom: Militaryace.

Page 14, bottom: Library of Congress.